T

The twentieth century is j
natives of Newlyn are rest
fishermen over Sunday ob
between rival towns, the a
Caught in the crossfire is Thomas Bolitho – merchant,
magistrate, mine owner and mayor – who respects the
fishermen's beliefs, but knows that riots are bad for
business. When he tries to play each end against the other,
both ends turn on him.

Nick Darke was born and raised in St Eval, Cornwall,
the son of a farmer. He trained as an actor and worked at
the Victoria Theatre, Stoke, throughout the 1970s. His first
play *Never Say Rabbit in a Boat*, about a group of Cornish
farmers who invest in a fishing net, was performed at the
Victoria Theatre in 1978, directed by Peter Cheeseman. He
has gone on to write over twenty plays which have been
produced by, amongst others, the RSC, National Theatre,
Royal Court, BBC radio and television. His work is
translated and performed regularly throughout the world.
He is a recipient of the George Devine Award and a Bard
of the Gorseth Kernow.

by the same author

Nick Darke Plays: One
The Dead Monkey
The King of Prussia
The Body
Ting Tang Mine

THE RIOT

Nick Darke

Methuen Drama

Copyright © 1999 by Nick Darke
The right of Nick Darke to be identified as the author of this work
has been asserted by him in
accordance with the Copyright, Designs and Patents Act, 1988

First published in Great Britain in 1999
by Methuen Publishing Limited
20 Vauxhall Bridge Road, London SW1V 2SA

Random House Australia (Pty) Limited
20 Alfred Street, Milsons Point, Sydney, New South Wales 2061, Australia

Random House New Zealand Limited
18 Poland Road, Glenfield, Auckland 10, New Zealand

Random House South Africa (Pty) Limited
Endulini, 5A Jubilee Road, Parktown 2193, South Africa

Methuen Publishing Limited Reg. No. 3543167

A CIP catalogue record for this book
is available from the British Library

Papers used by Methuen Publishing Ltd are natural, recyclable products made
from wood grown in sustainable forests. The manufacturing processes conform
to the environmental regulations of the country of origin.

ISBN 0–413–73730–6

Typeset by Deltatype Ltd, Birkenhead, Merseyside
Printed and bound in Great Britain by Cox & Wyman Ltd, Reading,
Berkshire

Caution

The Riot

for Jack Morgan and Trevor England

The Riot, a co-production between the Royal National Theatre and Kneehigh Theatre of Cornwall, premiered in the Cottesloe auditorium of the Royal National Theatre, London, on 4 February 1999. The cast was as follows:

Bolitho	Geoffrey Hutchings
Harriet Screetch	Emma Rice
Billy Triggs/Isreal Screetch	Tristan Sturrock
Borlase/Claude Mitchell	Charlie Barnecut
Capps/Spreckly/Mother	Terry Taplin
Tack Bazely	Carl Grose
Mrs Triggs	Sue Hill
Maude	Mary Woodvine
Sarah	Bec Applebee
Matthews/Jumbo/Carne	Roger Morlidge
Tot/Squincher	Mike Shepherd
Musician	Colin Seddon

Directed by Mike Shepherd
Designed by Bin Mitchell
Music by Jim Carey

Characters

Bolitho	**Tack**
Harriet Screetch	**Mrs Triggs**
Billy Triggs	**Maude**
Israel Screetch	**Sarah**
Borlase	**Matthews**
Claude Mitchell	**Jumbo**
Capps	**Carne**
Spreckly	**Tot**
Mother	**Squincher**

Sunday night.
May 1896.
A light on in Ebeneezer Chapel.
Inside, the congregation sing a hymn.
Tack Bazely *waits outside in the shadows.*

Hymn
> Will your anchor hold in the storms of life,
> When the clouds unfold their wings of strife?
> When the strong tides lift, and the cables strain,
> Will your anchor drift, or firm remain?

The chapel door opens and **Billy Triggs** *comes out.*
Tack emerges from the shadows.
The following scene is played over the hymn.

Billy   Oo's that?

Tack   'right Bill?

Billy   Tack.

Tack   We on?

Billy   Dawn tomorra. South Pier. Git the Pengelly boys,
Blewetts, Richards clan, Treneer brothers –

Tack *heads off.*

Billy   Tack!

Tack   What?

Billy   No Squincher.

Tack   Eh?

Billy   We dun't want violence Tack.

Tack   There's more to this than fishin Billy.

Billy   All we're gonna do is when the Yorky fleet ties up
we board em peaceful and tell em boys we've ad enough a
Sunday fishin. Then quiet as you like without a blow bein
struck we tip their catch in the arbour.

Tack   Oo's this?

Billy (*peers into shadows*)   Jumbo!

Tack   Yorky!

Enter **Jumbo** *walking fast.*
Tack *steps out and bars his route.*

Billy   Not fishin thun Jum.

Jumbo   No.

Tack   'doin ashore?

Jumbo   Sellin cheap tobacca.

Tack   Ah.

Billy *and* **Tack** *check no one's coming.*

Billy   What y'got?

Jumbo   Thick Black and Bogey Roll.

Billy   Gis 'alf a Bogey.

Jumbo *sells* **Billy** *half a pound of tobacco.*

Tack   Ounca Black.

Billy *fills his pipe.*
Jumbo *sells* **Tack** *an ounce of Black.*
Enter **Maude** *walking quickly.*

Billy   'right Maude?

Maude   'o Billy.

Tack   'Maude.

Maude   'Tack.

Exit **Maude**.
Exit **Jumbo** *in* **Maude**'*s direction.*

Hymn
 Will your anchor hold in the straits of fear,
 When the breakers roar and the reef is near?
 While the surges rave, and the wild winds blow,
 Shall the angry waves then your ship o'erflow?

Enter **Tot**, *an older man.*
Tack *retires to the shadows to light his pipe.*

Tot Whass on?

Billy (*filling his pipe*) Ullo Tot.

Tot Eh?

Billy Nothin much.

Tot Not what I eard.

Billy Ow d'ya mean?

Tot 'morra morning.

Billy What about it?

Tot Down Quay.

Billy Aw that.

Enter **Williams**.

Williams We on?

Billy Dawn. South Pier.

Williams Goo'boy.

Billy Alert Mousehole.

Williams Mousehole's 'lerted!

Exit **Williams**.

Tot Yorkies got as much right to fish ere as you ave.

Billy We dun't wanna stop em fishin.

Tot If you wan'earn their kinda money you go sea all week.

The chapel door opens.
Billy *dives.*
A woman stands framed in the doorway.

Mrs Triggs Billy! Where be to? Come back in ere and worship God! That you, Tot? Seen Bill?

Tot   No!

Exit **Mrs Triggs** *to chapel.*

Tot   Unlike you this is Billy. Why ya doin it?

Billy   I'm desperate Tot.

Tot   Hell for?

Billy   When I tell a girl that I take ome 'alf what a packer get, she laugh in me face.

Enter **Pascoe**.

Pascoe   Whass the signal.

Billy   Toldya the signal.

Pascoe   Barrel stave innit?

Billy   Yes.

Exit **Pascoe**.

Tot   There'll be limbs torn off and several deaths.

Billy   No Tot.

Tot   Squincher goin?

Billy   Squincher's took care of.

Tot   Oo by?

Billy   Tack.

Tack (*steps forward, smoking his pipe*)   'right Tot?

Tot   Hah!

Exit **Tot**.

Hymn
  Will your anchor hold in the floods of death,
  When the waters cold chill your latest breath?
  On the rising tide you can never fail,
  While your anchor holds within the veil . . .

Bolitho *walks his aged mother home from church.*
They walk as they speak.

Billy Evening Mr Bolitho.

Bolitho Not singin Billy.

Billy No sir.

Bolitho Why's that?

Billy 'ot as 'ellfire in that chapel.

Bolitho No breeze.

Billy Thass the killer.

Bolitho Would'n surprise me if they Yorkies as you call
em, out there now, fishin, desecratin the Sabbath, was busy
thanking God on this windless night for the gift of steam
propulsion.

Billy Those oo got it.

Bolitho Most Yorkies ave Billy.

Billy Guess so sir.

Mother Oo's that?

Bolitho Billy Triggs Mother!

Mother Eh?

Bolitho Mrs Trigg's boy Billy!

Mother Izze frisky?

Bolitho E's in want of air Mother!

Mother Thass no good to me.

Bolitho Eighty-seb'm year old and still 'opeful, eh, Bill?

Billy 'elluva lady sir.

Bolitho Always was. I wouldn' ave my wealth without er.
She gotta Rockerfella's 'ead for business. I owe 'alf my
fortune to this ole specimin. 'ard to believe eh Bill?

Exit **Bolitho** *and* **Mother**.
Tack *emerges from the shadows, smoking his pipe.*

Billy   Dawn.

Tack   South Pier.

Billy   No Squincher.

Tack   'right.

Billy   Make im swear an oath.

Tack   Oo's e with now?

Billy   Primitive Methodists?

Tack   E left em after e broke a circuit preacher's neck.

Billy   Weslyans?

Tack   They chucked 'im out when e demolished the chapel up Trevarrack.

Billy   Bible Christians.

Tack   Bible Christians took im on.

Billy   Bible Christian oath.

Tack   E won't break that.

Billy *goes back in the chapel.*
The final chorus of the hymn swells to a crescendo.

Hymn
   Will your eyes behold the morning light,
   The city of gold and the harbour bright?
   Will you anchor safe by the heavenly shore,
   When life's storms are passed for evermore?

It is topped by a blast from a steam whistle.

Dawn.
South Pier.
Steam and smoke from the Yorky drifters entering harbour.
Billy *stands on the dock wall counting boats with one hand, a barrel stave in the other.*

Pascoe *stands on the pier head, a rope in his hand.*
A thousand buccas stand the other end.

Market.
Backjowsters and packers assemble empty boxes and sample baskets.
Merchants open up their stalls.
A jowster walks across the market ringing a handbell.
Merchants mark up their starting prices on boards.
Packers haul boxes across the market floor.
Jowsters pitch sample baskets up on to the wall.
Salt and ice are hauled into the market.

Pier.
Billy *stops counting and approaches the buccas.*

Billy   We gotta get through this without a blow bein
struck. Yorkies arn't the Penzance gang oo we fight any
day of the week. We drink with Yorkies. We buy tobacco
off Yorkies. We got no quarrel wi' Yorkies bar the Sunday
fishin! Damme Yorkies don't even wanna fish Sundays tis
the buyers make em do it. We outnumber em so they in't
gonna start nothing. (*To* **Tack**.) Any sign a Squincher?

Tack (*after a cursory look around*)   Nope.

Voice 1 (*off*)   Billy!

Billy   What?

Voice 1 (*off*)   Would it elp if we sung 'ymn?

Billy   Sing 'ymn if ya want Peter.

Voice 1 (*off*)   If I sung 'ymn twould stop me 'ittin em!

Voice 2 (*off*)   Wouldn' stop them 'ittin you!

A distant yell.

Billy (*to* **Tack**)   That Squincher?

Another yell.

Tack   E swore!

Billy   Did e?

Tack   Yes!

Billy   When I give the signal start boardin. Twenty men to a vessel. Wait for the signal.

Billy *runs to the Bull's Nose.*
Squincher*'s yells get closer.*

Billy   Pascoe! Chain the gaps!

Pascoe *hauls the rope.*
Billy *holds the barrel stave aloft.*
A Yorky Skipper appears at the top of a ladder, a mooring rope in his hand. He hauls the rope towards a bollard and makes it fast.

Skipper   Fook's goin on?!

Billy   There's no landing in this port today jack.

Skipper   Eh?

Billy   Your fish is goin overboard –

Tack (*indicates the buccas*)   And I 'vise ya not to speak else you go with em.

Squincher*'s yells get closer.*

Billy   Tack! Go in the market. Send the packers off and all the merchants.

Exit **Tack**.

(*To* **Skipper**.) Sooner we git the job done you boys can go ashore and take some breakfast.

A blood-curdling yell, off, signifies **Squincher***'s imminence.*
Billy *brings the barrel stave down like a scimitar in a great swoop.*

Tally ho boys!

A thousand buccas swarm down ladders and board the Yorky boats.
Enter **Squincher** *with a merchant's sales hut on his back.*
The hut bears the legend 'Arnold Capps and Son, Fishmerchant, Lowestoft'.
Capps, *inside the hut, unseen except for his legs, struggles to wrest control from* **Squincher**.

Billy   Squincher!

Squincher, *the hut on his back, walks up and down the pier like a giant demented crab looking for a space between boats in the harbour to drop the hut.*
Capps *hangs on, protesting loudly.*

Squincher   Sorry Billy I just gotta ditch this f'ker in the 'arbour then I'll –

Billy   You swore an oath.

Squincher   Thass all I'm gonna do boy then I'll f'k off ome.

Market.
Enter **Tack**.

Tack   Vacate the market!

Packer   Eh?

Tack   Buyin's cancelled! (*Picking up sample baskets.*) Clear the boxes!

Pier.

Billy   I said no violence!

Squincher   I'm f'kin with e on that one Billy all the f'kin way!

Tack   We've had a bellyful of Sunday fishin. We're a God-fearin Nonconformist people. We observe the Sabbath.

Tack *scatters the baskets and starts to fold a merchant's stall.*

Merchant   Oy!

Tack   New bucca's rules, cap'm, Sunday's fish is null and void.

Billy   You know oo this is?

Squincher   F'kin Capps Billy I 'ate the bastard. I could'n f'kin elp meself, Billy!

Market.

Tack (*dragging bags of salt across the floor chased by a backjowster*) Stow your salt and ice dear there id'n no market today!

Billy Put im down!

Squincher Said to meself aw, aww, awww! Just the one f'kin . . . one li' . . . f'kin . . . Squinch!

Billy (*shouting up inside the booth*) Sorry Mr Capps I did me best to prevent this!

Squincher *shoots the hut into the harbour.*
Billy *hangs on to Capps's legs.*
Capps *is revealed, fuming,* **Billy** *at his feet.*

Squincher Thass it Billy. I'm omeward. Good luck boy. Seegin.

Exit **Squincher**.
Capps *and* **Billy** *survey the scene in the harbour.*
Pascoe *shackles the chain-end to the mooring ring.*
Billy *keeps his eye on* **Capps** *at the same time guarding* **Pascoe**.
The odd clear shout across water in the stillness of dawn.

Billy 'e swore an oath to stay off the quay –

Capps Reaper. Thirteen thousand.

Billy – and there's no bugger in this port dread the wrath of God more'n Squincher Mr Capps.

Capps Ocean Dawn. Eight thousand . . .

Billy So 'e must 'ave damn good reason, don't you think?

Capps *Succeed* six, *Osprey* nine, *Lotus* five, *Rosebud* six, *Bessie* four thousand fish . . . Rice and Chapman's boats eight thousand each twenty-four . . . *Boy Victor* . . . six thousand. (*Pointing as he calculates.*) . . . fifteen, three, eight, four, twelve . . . (*Calculating.*) . . . hundred and eight . . . fourteen shillings per . . . (*Calculates.*) . . . six hundred and forty-three pounds!

Exit **Capps**.

Hymn
>Behold! Behold the morning light!
>City of gold! Harbour bright!
>Anchor close to the tempestuous shore,
>The storm is here! Now! For evermore!

A single mackerel rises in the air and lands centre stage.

Bolitho's *kitchen.*
Overlooking Mount's Bay, doors to garden, house and scullery.
Maude *sits at the table and polishes silver.*
Enter **Mrs Triggs, Borlase, Inspector Matthews** *and* **Harriet Screetch**.

Mrs Triggs (*to* **Maude**)   Fetch Bolitho. And 'urry. Tis urgent. Urgent. There's hell up down arbour tell im.

Exit **Maude** *to garden.*

Stand there. (*Grooming* **Harriet**.) Gotta be clean if you wanna work in this kitchen. Call im Mister at all times and curtsey when e come in the room. Curtsey, canne?

Harriet *attempts a curtsey.*

Mrs Triggs   Thass a squat! Curtsey's 'alf way. Try again . . . stop! If e speak to ya talk back clear but not loud and no blasphemin. We don't ave no crudity down ere. Whass your name?

Harriet   'arriet Screetch.

Mrs Triggs   Speak up. Don't mumble.

Harriet (*shouts*)   'arriet Screetch.

Mrs Triggs   Too loud. Mr Borlase, whass your name?

Borlase   Mr Borlase.

Mrs Triggs (*to* **Harriet**)   See? Where y'from?

Borlase   St Just.

Mrs Triggs   Not you!

Harriet   Botallack.

Mrs Triggs   Eh?!

Harriet   Botallack!

Mrs Triggs   Dun't speak. 'less your spoken to cus you
never knaw oo tis. We ad a duchess in ere Wednesday.
Damn duchess. Stood where you are now. She said call
me Your Grace cus I'm a duchess so you gotta be careful.
I said after I said I knew twas a duchess cus I could smell
er. And the fragrance lingered summin rotten. Thass what
tis like ere. Damme there's times when this place is awash
with nobility. Viscounts, earls cus e's the Lord what is it?

Borlase   Lord Lieutenant.

Mrs Triggs   That mean when the Queen idn ere e's
Queen.

Borlase   Hardly.

Mrs Triggs   Near enough. Judges. There's bin more
judges scuttled across this floor'n rats cus e's whaddycallem?

Borlase   High Sheriff.

Mrs Triggs   E build arbours. E shut down mines. E
cultivate broccoli. There's nothin grown, made, extracted
or caught from the Land's End to Bodmin Town what id'n
boiled up and brewed in this ere very kitchen. Nothin goin
on what dun't emanate from Bolitha. Nothin goin on at
all.

Enter **Bolitho** *and* **Maude**.
Maude *continues polishing silver.*

Bolitho   What's goin on?

Mrs Triggs   Hell up.

Bolitho (*to* **Matthews**)   Yes?

Mrs Triggs   I said it would happen. Tis the heat.
'undred thousand mackerel restored to their natural
element.

Bolitho   By who?

Matthews   Our fishermen.

Mrs Triggs   A power of em, thousand? Marched on the pier, boarded the Yorky men's boats and chucked Sunday's catch in the 'arbour.

Bolitho   You were there?

Mrs Triggs   They was. Am I right?

Borlase   There's chaos down there Mr Bolitho.

Matthews   I've never seen nothin like it.

Mrs Triggs   Acres and acres of dead wasted fish. The stench this weather. Plump. Big. Full of oil.

Bolitho   Can't you stop em, Inspector Matthews?

Mrs Triggs   'course e can't stop em! Im'n three constables and Mr Borlase ere, what are ya?

Borlase   Magistrate's clerk –

Mrs Triggs   Against a thousand buccas?

Bolitho   Who's king of all this?

Matthews (*accusing*)   Her son.

Mrs Triggs (*proud*)   William.

Bolitho (*astonished*)   Billy?

Matthews   William Triggs.

Bolitho   Billy Triggs!?

Borlase   Hopping e was from vessel to vessel –

Bolitho (*to* **Maude**)   Fetch me hat and coat.

Exit **Maude**.

Mrs Triggs   – checkin they was light of fish –

Borlase   Stood up like a Matabele in the prow.

Matthews   'zactly like a Matabele.

Borlase   Statued like a tribesman with a barrel stave in his hand.

Mrs Triggs   A barrel stave?

Borlase   Aye.

Mrs Triggs   The little bugger!

Exit **Mrs Triggs**.

Bolitho (*pacing*)   Are the public houses shut?

Matthews   All but the Union.

Bolitho   Who's with the buccas? Mousehole?

Matthews   Yes, sir.

Bolitho   Porthleven?

Matthews   Solid behind em.

Bolitho   Penzance?

Matthews   Neutral.

Bolitho   My ass! What's your full strength Inspector?

Matthews   Jack Tamblyn.

Bolitho   One?

Matthews   That's the way it's lookin.

Bolitho   What about Tony Sim?

Matthews   Tony Sim was 'it be a cricket ball Saturday, got knocked out, we can't wake im.

Bolitho   Is e alive?

Matthews   O yes sir he's talkin, we just can't wake im.

Bolitho   Ted Richards?

Matthews   Richards threw off 'is uniform and joined the buccas.

Borlase   Ted got seven brothers fishin Mr Bolitho.
Blood's thicker than water.

Bolitho   So. Jack Tamblyn. 'ow's 'is leg?

Matthews   Still in irons.

Bolitho   Can e walk?

Matthews   E can but it take im time to get goin.

Bolitho   Telegraph Camborne for reinforcements.

Matthews   Yes sir.

Bolitho   Every man they can spare. Recruit Specials. Men oo can walk.

Matthews *makes his way to the door.*

Bolitho   Let it be known I shall speak outside the ice plant in one hour's time.

Matthews   Ice plant.

Bolitho   Matthews.

Matthews   Sir?

Bolitho   Capture Triggs.

Exit **Matthews**.

Maude, where's me hat and coat!

Enter **Capps**.

Capps   Not so fast Bolitho.

Bolitho   I'm a busy man Mr Capps.

Capps   I won't beat about the bush.

Bolitho   Can't see you now.

Capps   I demand compensation.

Bolitho   The fault is yours.

Capps   Six hundred and forty-three pounds.

Bolitho   Before this season started our fishermen travelled East and begged you buyers to respect the Sabbath in this port. All agreed to a universal ban on Sunday fishin, all of em, bar one.

Capps That's –

Bolitho (*enraged*) Don't deny it!

Capps You can't allow God to intercede in business!

Bolitho E's the only bugger you can.

Enter **Maude** *with hat and coat.*

Capps I worship too Bolitho.

Bolitho I find that 'ard to believe.

Capps My god is mackerel, market day is Mass and I'm the ruddy Pope and when the Pope is barred from Rome e buggers off to Plymouth.

Bolitho Plymouth?

Capps Next year I shall take my business to Plymouth where they've heard of neither God nor Sunday.

Bolitho Don't be so damned hasty.

Capps My property's destroyed, I've been publicly disgraced and denied the basic human right to trade in fish.

Bolitho Tis a protest nothin more.

Capps You condone it do you?

Bolitho No sir. Don't try to catch me out. These men are decent people. They've bin driven to it. Your boats go sea Saturday shoot away off the Wolf, stay out Sunday and come ashore Monday with two-day-old fish. They id'n even overs they're over overs. Raff fish they're sellin fourteen bob undred! There's not another market all week where you can get alf that price for dayboat fish! I'm a businessman too and ruthless with it but there's one thing and one thing only that I will place beyond the sanctity of cash. Fear of God.

Capps For a steam drifter Plymouth is no distance at all.

Bolitho If you go to Plymouth this port will die.

Capps *stands firm.*

Bolitho *offers him a seat.*
They sit across the table.

Capps   I want the army.

Bolitho   I've sent to Camborne for police reinforcements
and we're drafting Specials.

Capps   I said the army.

Bolitho   That's absurd.

Capps   Regular soldiers.

Bolitho   For God's sake allow me the chance to talk to
our boys first.

Capps   I want justice, Bolitho.

Bolitho   You'll get justice!

Capps   And compensation for two dozen boats who lost
their catch. The full market value of a hundred thousand
fish. The Monday market value.

Bolitho (*to* **Maude**)   Fetch me a pen.

Capps   Six hundred and forty-three pounds.

Bolitho   Gross?

Capps   Aye.

Bolitho   You're not payin packagin are ya? Cartage? Ice?
Eh?

Capps   No.

Bolitho   I'll give ya six undred pound.

Harriet's *jaw drops.*

Capps   That'll do.

Maude *places writing equipment on the table and* **Bolitho** *sits to
write the cheque.* **Maude** *sits and resumes polishing silver.*

Bolitho   That conclude worship for today.

Capps   No sir. Not quite.

Bolitho   Eh?

Capps   There's eighteen boats still at sea. Full of mackerel. Those fish have to be landed.

Bolitho   Wait til tomorra Mr Capps.

Capps   I want facilities made ready for them today at Penzance.

Bolitho   Penzance.

Capps   Yes.

Bolitho (*blotting the cheque*)   You're aware of the enmity that exists between the two ports?

Capps   That's no concern of mine.

Bolitho   The blind hatred of near neighbours?

Capps   It doesn't bother me.

Bolitho   There'll be a bloodbath.

Capps   That depends.

Bolitho   On what?

Capps   On how soon the army gets here.

Bolitho   Borlase.

Borlase   Sir?

Bolitho   Go to the railway terminus. Instruct Mr Rogers to clear the downline of all trains, then telegraph Devonport Barracks to despatch a battalion poste haste.

Borlase   Yes sir.

Bolitho   I shall be at the ice plant.

Exit **Borlase**.

(*Handing the cheque to* **Capps**.) That do ya?

Capps (*pocketing cheque*)   Aye. For now.

Exit **Capps**.

Bolitho Oo's done this Maude, oo's at the back of it eh!? Triggs? No! Billy? I can't believe it! Put the port at risk like that. We nearly 'ad this Sunday business sorted out! 'ad Capps in the bag! One more season! There's more to this than fishin Maude, oh yes more, much more (*Putting on his hat.*) and I gotta putta stop to it before –

Enter **Sarah**.

Sarah Bin a massacre.

Bolitho What?

Sarah Undreds dead.

Bolitho Where?

Sarah Bulawayo.

Bolitho Thank God for that.

Exit **Bolitho**.

Maude *throws down the silver, takes a plug of Bogey Roll from her apron pocket, puts her feet up on the table and fills a pipe.*

Sarah (*hunting for things to eat*) I couldn't rouse 'is mother. She might be dead but I left er breakfast with er 'case she wake up peckish. (*Watching* **Maude** *light her pipe.*) Bin wi' Jumbo? (*No reply.*) Down quay? (*No reply.*) Last night? (*No reply.*) Filthy bitch.

Maude *smokes.*

Maude Didn't say did and I didn't say didn't did I.

Sarah Didn't means did.

Maude Didn't say didn't.

Sarah Didn't say it but ya meant it.

Maude Didn't say nothin.

Sarah Nothin mean didn't and didn't mean did.

Maude All mean did to you dun it.

Sarah Well did ya?

Maude   Yes!

Sarah   Filthy bitch.

Maude   I'll go again tonight.

Sarah   If e id'n dead.

Exit **Sarah**.

Maude (*offering pipe*)   Smoke? (*Handing* **Harriet** *pipe*.) Keep your mouth shut.

Harriet   ?

Maude   'bout Jumbo.

Harriet *inhales and chokes*.

Maude   Too strong for ya? Yorky tobacca thass why. Come across from Russia. Duty-free. Bogey Roll. Best there is. Don't get Black. Black'll kill ya. Black's deadly. Black's black as a dog's gut. Tis only good for chewin but they d'smoke it. Jumbo. Porky. Spindle. Tin Tack. Cronjie. Yorky boys.

They smoke.

Harriet   Go wi' Yorkies, do ya?

Maude   No. One Yorky. Jumbo. All right?

Harriet   Yes.

Maude   Good.

They smoke.
Harriet *gets the hang of it*.

Harriet   Thass where me brothers is.

Maude   Russia?

Harriet   Bulawayo.

A short burst of African drumming.

Harriet   Israel?!

Maude   Eh?

Harriet   E's the dead one.

She sings.

Israel, in thy youthful prime
Hast leapt the bounds of time,
Suddenly from earth released:
Taken to an early rest,
Caught into eternity
I wish you was down ere with me.

Maude   How did e die?

Harriet   Bolitha killed im.

Maude (*shocked*)   What?

Harriet   Yes.

Maude   How?

Harriet   Botallack Mine shut down. Me brothers took
work in Bulawayo. Israel died

Maude   So Bolitha didn –

Harriet   Yes e did! Dun't didn-did me!

Maude   But e didn –

Harriet   Bloody Queen knaw all about it.

Maude   Eh?

Maude   Yeah e was mentioned in despatches.

African drums.
Buckingham Palace.

Courtier (Borlase)   Colonel Spreckly, Your Majesty.
Gifford's 'orse.

Queen Victoria (Bolitho) *inclines her head.*

Spreckly (Capps, *kneeling*)   A battle near Bulawayo,
Ma'am.
Over three hundred mortalities.

Queen Victoria   Yes?

Courtier   Tell 'er Majesty all about it.

Spreckly   On Saturday morning last a battalion of
troopers under my command was sent to look for rebels.
We found em! My men crossed the Donga, opened out in
skirmishing order and charge!

*Two hundred troopers on horseback gallop through the bush. The
drumming increases.*

Spreckly   The natives fled. Rifles were discarded by my
men who used revolvers for close-quarter work.

Revolvers are drawn from inside tunics –

We shot em up trees, in bushes, down 'oles. Four
hundred rebels were killed outright.

Queen   Any –

Spreckly   Fatalities on our side?

Victoria *inclines her head.*

Spreckly   Yes, Ma'am. One. As plucky a little bugger as
I've had privilege to command. But e was a conscript
Ma'am, recruited over there from the mining community,
so e ain't cost us nothin.

Victoria   Name him.

Spreckly   Screetch. Israel Screetch. He was advancing at
the head of a column on the westward side. Driving the
enemy back with his revolver. A hidden native –

*High up a Matabele can be seen holding an assegai aloft, poised,
muscles tense. The Matabele hurls the assegai.*

Spreckly   Through the neck Ma'am.

Israel *falls at* **Harriet**'s *feet, a spear through his neck.*

Harriet (*heart-rending*)   Israel!

Maude   Bolitha didn' kill im!

Harriet   Yes e did!

Maude   E didn' chuck the spear.

Harriet   E shut Botallack!

Enter **Billy**.
His garnsey is splattered with blood.
His face is covered and his hair matted with blood.
He carries a barrel stave.

Billy   Matey picked a fight wi' Clemo in the Union. They beat the shit out ob'm –

Maude   Who?

Billy   Yorky chap e argued wid about the fishin, Clemo scat'n one and e didn't knaw e was a cripple cus e's from Mousehole so the Yorky it'n back and that was it.

Maude   What the hell is a Yorky doing in the Union?

Billy   (*lifting the hem of his garnsey, several packets of tobacco drop to the floor*)   Sellin this.

Maude   (*picking up tobacco*)   Jumbo!

Billy   Know im? (*Removing garnsey and handing it to* **Harriet**.) Stick this in the slab will ya?

Harriet   Cook it?

Billy   Burn it!

Harriet *does as she's told.*
Billy *pours water and washes his face and head.*

Maude   Where's e to?

Billy   Claude Mitchell's place. Next door to the Union they took im in.

Maude *hunts about for bandages, linament, iodine etc.*

Maude   Out the pub?

Billy   Dragged im off the street.

Maude   Claude don't drink.

Billy   I said, off the street.

Maude   Off the street? Is e dead?

Billy (*washing*) E should be. They was yellin –

Voice – crucify the bastard!

Billy (*in amongst the crowd, fending them off* **Jumbo**) Leave im be!

Voice Murder the sod!

Billy I said no bloodshed!

Matthews *stands by watching as* **Billy** *crawls out from under the crowd, nursing his knuckles.*

Billy (*washing*) Copper there just stood'n watched.

Maude That 'is blood?

Billy Where?

Maude On you.

Billy No!

Maude You beat im?

Billy I never beat im!

Maude You stole 'is tobacca.

Billy Ab'm stole the bloody stuff I kept it for'n I picked up all I could the bloody Union's packed out I was on me' ands and knees, crushed! That 'ot I couldn' breath (*Half bent, head dripping, hands out.*) Gotta towel?

Maude Oo's blood is it?

Billy (*to* **Harriet**) Would you go out the servants yard and find a basket with a blue garnsey in it please.

Exit **Harriet**.

Maude Who's blood?

Billy Mine!

Maude Oo hit ya?

Mrs Triggs (*hitting him with barrel stave*) I told you not to carry any weapons!

Billy (*cowering*) I'm not!

Mrs Triggs What d'ya call this?

Enter **Harriet** *with the blue garnsey.*

Harriet Copper!

Maude Up the stairs –

Billy Where's me –

Maude (*handing him barrel stave*) – hide in a bedroom.

Exit **Billy** *to house.*
Exit **Maude**.
Enter **Matthews** *from garden. His head is bandaged.*

Matthews Where's Triggs?

Harriet Triggs?

Matthews Aye.

Harriet Which?

Matthews Which? William!

Harriet Whass e done?

Matthews Assault and Battery.

Harriet On who?

Matthews (*spies tobacco*) 'hell's this?

Harriet Thick Black and thass the Bogey Roll. Black's black as a dog's gut. Tis only good for chewin.

Matthews Yours?

Harriet No.

Matthews Whose?

Harriet Er . . .

Matthews Staff.

Harriet Yes.

Matthews Where are they?

Harriet Down Riot.

Matthews All of em?

Harriet Yes sir.

Matthews Where did they get it?

Harriet What?

Matthews 'bacca.

Harriet Oo?

Matthews Staff!

Harriet Don't know sir.

Matthews What d'you mean you don't know? What d'ya mean? Don't know? Don't know? Y'mean you don't know where you get this? Who you buy it off? Eh?!

Harriet Yorky.

Matthews Yes! And that Yorky was beat to atoms by William Triggs.

Harriet No e wad'n.

Matthews Was you there? No! I was. I got this for my troubles. Fishbox done that. I'll run im to ground like the animal e is and when I do e'll get no quarter.

Exit **Matthews**.

African drums.
Harriet *takes a coin wrapped in paper from her pockets. She unwraps the coin and reads what's written on the paper.*

Israel (**Billy**) Dearest sister, here's a guilder stamped out of ore raised from the snakepit they call a copper mine where me and the boys is workin. The army doles out guilders when you sign up to conquer the Matabele on Saturdays insteada playin cricket. Its value is an English shillin. Bin down Bolitha's yet? Ole bitch Triggs'll get y'work if you curtsey at er right and call im Mister. All my love,

Harriet Israel!

Enter **Sarah**.

Sarah (*taking carving knives, cleavers etc. out of drawers, off hooks, and making a pile on the table*) Army's comin now. Royal Berkshires. Knaw their last postin?

Harriet Africa?

Sarah (*gathering weapons*) Ireland. Eviction duty. Trained to fight the Celtic nations. HMS *Banshee*'s set sail from Plymouth.

Harriet Where's e headed?

Sarah Where d'ya think? Just up-anchored'n out. (*Finding a sack to put the weaponry in.*) Yeah, scared stiff a we.

Harriet Whass all this for?

Sarah What d'ya think?

Harriet Stabbin Yorkies?

Sarah No.

Harriet Penzance.

Sarah They got worse'n this.

Harriet If the Army catch ya they'll shoot y'like a Matabele.

Sarah (*her sack full*) Bloody army catch me they'll get it in the gut. (*At the door.*) Comin?

Harriet No.

Sarah Scared?

Harriet No.

Sarah C'mon.

Harriet Stayin ere.

Sarah Why?

Harriet　Tid'n Penzance you wanna bother with. There's people starvin all over the county not just ere while Bolitha's grown fat. Bolitha paid out six undred to the Yorky bloke I saw im do it.

Sarah　I knaw all about Bolitha. I'm comin back for e. With a rope.

Exit **Sarah**.
Enter **Billy**.
He carries a breakfast tray with a newspaper and boiled egg, uneaten, on it.

Billy　I think the old mother's passed on.

Harriet　You're in the shit.

Billy　Oo with?

Harriet　Assault and battery.

Billy　I was tryin to fend em off! Bloody copper.

Harriet　Bolitha set im on ya.

Billy　Bolitha?

Harriet　Yes!

Billy　Where's e gone?

Harriet　Ice plant.

Exit **Billy**.
Enter **Borlase**. *Perspiring and breathless.*

Borlase　Downline's clear and I telegraphed the military. (*Removing his jacket.*) Excuse me, ran all the way from Penzance. I can't tell you the relief I felt when I walked from here to the station and not one person noticed me. For a magistrate's clerk in a town like Penzance that's something of a miracle. I honestly thought that I was going to be lynched. When I walked out of this door I could feel the noose around my neck. Did you know there's three ropewalks between here and Penzance? I avoided them all. There was a clamour in Market Jew Street but Carne's Bank's gone bust and twas nothing more than anxious investors. O yes, by and large Penzance is tranquil as ever

it was which is lively enough for a man of my disposition.
Even the station is silent and empty of trains.

Enter **Bolitho**.

Bolitho Borlase! Where've ya bin?

Borlase Penzance sir –

Bolitho I told y'to get to the ice plant –

Borlase Sir you said –

A sharp extrusion of steam.

Bolitho They accused me of sellin this port!

Ice plant.
A huge extrusion of steam envelops **Bolitho**.

Bolitho I got to the plant as they was freezin the last ton
of ice bound for Penzance. There's no ice without steam
Borlase and I was shrouded in the stuff.

A loud hiss and a cloud of vapour.
A lump of ice drops from a hopper, slides down a shute and lands at
Bolitho*'s feet.*
Revealed: women dressed in overcoats and mittens operating handles.
Bolitho *stands on the ice block.*
Sarah *runs past (unseen by* **Bolitho***) with the sack of knives.*

Bolitho The women shut down the cooling furnace and
the vapours dispersed.

The steam reveals a hundred buccas arrayed in front of **Bolitho**.
Every bucca has a knife in his hand.
Sarah*'s sack is empty.*

Bolitho I was surrounded by buccas. And they each held
a knife.

Borlase O my God!

Bolitho I knew every one by sight.

Borlase Every bucca?

Bolitho No. Every knife. Where the hell did ya get my
cutlery!

Enter **Billy**.

Billy   Mr Bolitho!

Bolitho   You!

Billy   No!

Bolitho   I'm damned disappointed Billy!

Billy   I gotta talk to ya!

Enter **Matthews**.

Bolitho   Catch im Matthews!

Billy *skips and sidles amongst the buccas snatching knives back where he can.*

Billy \ Call this copper off!

Bolitho   Abusing your mother's position!

Billy   Let me explain.

Bolitho   Yes Billy. Tomorra! Before the bench.

Exit **Billy** *with knives, chased by* **Matthews**.

Bolitho   Boy Bazely. Know im?

Borlase   Tack?

Bolitho   Bugger's a communist.

Tack   Where's the ice goin Mr Bolitho?

Bolitho   Penzance.

Tack   Why?

Bolitho   There's Yorky boats still at sea. They got fish to land. They can't land em so they're takin em to Penzance. They require ice to pack em with.

Tack   Where's our compensation Bolitha?

Bolitho   Compensation –

Tack We deserve it don't ya think?

Bolitho How the hell did e know 'bout that?

Tack Come on Bolitha we want the truth.

Bolitho Yes. I paid out compensation.

Tack Oo to?

Bolitho A Yorky buyer.

Tack Capps.

Bolitho Yes.

Sarah Six undred pound.

Bolitho Goddammit Borlase the bugger knew ow much! That's money out me own damn pocket what I've spent on your behalf.

Voice On my behalf?

Bolitho Yes!

Voice I'll ave it back!

Tack What about Strick?

Bolitho I'd bin to the harbour office and ordered Strick to put to sea, intercept the Yorky boats and divert em to Penzance.

Tack Was that another deal you struck with Capps?

Bolitho Yes! E's clever Bazely I'll give im that, in a devious sorta way. E challenged my motive see? Threw me back on the defensive.

Tack Thank you, Mr Bolitho. Most kind of ya. Sold the port. Sold the people. We do appreciate that don't we men.

Bolitho We got the nineteen undreds comin up. Do you want the nineteen undreds to pass ya by and dock in Plymouth? Cus that's what'll appen if you drive Capps up there. This is a great port but without buyers we're nothin! The Yorky fleet is four-fifths steam! They can make

Plymouth in a fraction of the time it take to sail there.
Plymouth's nothin to them! And if they land to Plymouth
the herring men will land to Plymouth. The cod will land
to Plymouth. The mid-watermen, the crabbers will land to
Plymouth. They'll all, all of em! Land to Plymouth and this
port will wither and die! Capps said to me if Penzance
wad'n made available to im next year e'd go Plymouth. I
warned im about your loathing for Penzance but e was
adamant. So I had no choice. I don't want to see you out
of a job, Tack. I don't want to see the port die. That is
why I put more time and effort into keepin it alive, Tack,
as alderman, mayor, 'arbour commissioner, magistrate, than
into me own damn business! So don't ever accuse me,
Tack, of sellin the people. I remember back in '78, Jaco
Bazely's boat *The Nipper* was smashed up in a storm,
'member that, Tack? No, you wouldn't cus you wad'n born
but sure 'nuff your daddy's swung you on 'is knee and told
y'about it. Twas that storm and the boats we lost that
convinced me of the need of a North Pier. I poured ten
thousand pounds of me own money into its construction so
our fishermen could sleep at night in the knowledge their
boats was safely harboured. So Tack, don't ever accuse me
of selling this port, Tack, I built it!

Voice There's a fleet of Yorkies rounding the Point!

Tack Where they headed?

Voice Penzance!

Sarah Come on boys!

The buccas stay put.

Tack E dun't give a damn about fishermen! No
businessman ever doled up six undred pound on behalf of
somebody else! Would you? Bolitha wouldn'! E's a
businessman!

Bolitho If you love this port, if you care for this town, if
you wanna ride out the old century on the backa prosperity
with hope at your heels stand back and give this ice free
passage to Penzance.

Bolitho *alights from the ice.*

Tack Bolitha built the North Pier. Bolitha poured ten thousand of 'is own money into it for our benefit e says. 'as it made us buccas rich, boys? No! Is Bolitha wealthy? Yes!

Bolitho Tack Bazely's determined, I'll give im that.

Tack You betrayed us Bolitha. You'll pay the price!

Bolitho E'll go to the Union and tip out all the drunks. Soon as one lot goes the other lot will foller.

Borlase What about the ice?

Tack Smash it men!

Borlase O my God.

Bolitho Now thun, I want you to do as I ask for once.

Borlase I did! I went to the terminus! I cleared the downline –

Bolitho Go back to the terminus –

Borlase (*heading for door*) O yes!

Bolitho Clear the upline –

Borlase The upline –

Bolitho I want a train with fish wagons prepared for departure. I want the packing station manned. Then go to Penzance quay and instruct the harbour master on my orders to make provision for three Yorky agents – Uttings, Thirkles and Capps. Got that?

Borlase (*on his way to the door*) Uttings, Thirkles and Capps – Uttings, Thirkles and Capps –

Bolitho And Borlase –

Borlase (*at door*) Sir?

Bolitho Take care of yourself.

Exit **Borlase**, *feeling his neck.*

Bolitho   Right. Where's me dinner?

Harriet   Your mother's bad Mister.

Bolitho   Mother's what?

Harriet   Bad.

Bolitho   Bad? How bad?

Harriet   It could be she's bad as it gets, Mister, but it might be she's better than that but if it is it id'n much. Mister.

Bolitho   Fix me dinner.

Exit **Bolitho**.

Harriet   E'll get bugger all outa me till e gimme a job. Bugger can starve like the rest of us.

Enter **Maude** *and* **Jumbo**.
Jumbo*'s face is badly damaged.*

Maude   Clear the table.

Harriet   What's this?

Maude   Jumbo. (*Laying* **Jumbo** *on the table.*) E was in Claude's place next door to the Union. We could hardly hear ourselves think –

Claude Mitchell*'s place.*

An excited racket coming through the wall from the Union next door. The frequent sound of breaking glass.
Maude *bandages* **Jumbo**.
Claude *nervously unwraps a plug of tobacco.*

Maude   Every now and again somebody would remember Jumbo –

Loud knockin on door (locked).
Claude *jumps.*

Voice (*off*)   Where's the Yorker!

Claude *crosses himself and prays.*

Voice (*off*)   Claude!

Voice (*off*)   Bring im out ere!

Voice (*off*)   Lynch the bastard!

Voice (*off*)   Whip im!

Voice (*off*)   Stick im on the treadmill!

Voice (*off*)   Transport im!

Claude (*holding up tobacco*)   Bogey or Black?

Maude   One or the other.

The clamour, off, persists.

Claude   O well. I don't drink. I don't chew tobacca. But if I get an opportunity to smoke it, in times of stress, I will take it. (*He fills a pipe with shaking hands.*) Such close proximity to a public house is a permanent temptation for a devout Methodist like myself. (*Lighting up.*) Christ spent forty days in the desert. (*Smoking.*) I've had forty years adjacent to the Union and I'm proud to say that, like Christ, I have never succu – (*the strength of the Black hits the back of his throat.*) – huinghh! Jeee – (*Rasping.*) What is thiss . . . ?

Maude   That's the Black.

Claude   Gimme water!

Maude (*looking round*)   Where?

Claude   Tis that thick with people out there I've bin unable to get to the bowser.

Maude   I'll go Union.

Claude   I didn't hear that.

Maude   Tis only water.

She unlocks the door, slips out, **Claude** *shuts it and draws the bolt.*

Maude   So I went in the Union –

Landlord   What!?

Maude   Water!

Landlord (*shouting above the din*)   Water!? In this weather!?

Maude   All they had was gin.

The **Landlord** *hands her gin.*
She knocks on the door.

Maude (*outside door*)   Claude!

Claude *unbolts the door and lets her in, shutting and bolting it fast. She passes gin to* **Claude**.

Maude   Gargle with it.

Claude *takes a mouthful of gin, throws his head back and starts to gargle.*

Maude   Shh!

Claude *pauses mid-gargle.*
Silence.

Maude   Hear that?

She opens the door wide and looks out, up and down the street.

Place is deserted. And I asked this kid, boy Giddy, where's everybody gone?

Giddy (*off*)   Bridge.

Maude   I'm gonna take me chance. Carry off Jumbo. (*Slapping* **Claude**'*s back.*) Thanks Claude!

Claude *swallows the gin, chokes, falls to his knees, and prays.*

Harriet   E'll ave to swallow boilin' water now to purify 'is gut.

Maude   Tis that or everlasting hell.

Harriet   I know which I'd prefer.

Enter **Mrs Triggs**.

Mrs Triggs   Where's Bolitha?

Harriet *points at the ceiling.*

Mrs Triggs With 'is mother?

Harriet *nods.*

Mrs Triggs Arn't surprised.

Maude She might be dead.

Mrs Triggs If this heat don't kill er nothin will. (*Tidying* **Harriet**.) Look at you! There's bin a damned duchess stood on that spot!

Harriet I can smell er.

Mrs Triggs (*standing back and surveying* **Harriet**) Gotta son your age oo's single.

Maude Hah!

Maude *is preparing* **Bolitho**'s *dinner.*

Mrs Triggs (*indicates* **Jumbo**) Who is this. (*She lowers the cover and looks at his face.*) E the one oo gotta beatin?

Harriet *nods.*

Mrs Triggs Whass e doin ere? How d'e get ere?

Harriet *inclines her head towards* **Maude**.

Mrs Triggs Maude! What is your interest in this man?

Maude Nothin to do with you.

Mrs Triggs You turned down William for this Yorky!

Maude I don't like William.

Mrs Triggs Like the Yorky do ya?

Maude I love im.

Mrs Triggs My son is down there riskin his life in dispute with these men. Is that all you can do to repay im? Treachery! I got you this job cus you was starvin. You was dressed in bal shag. Billy looked at you and e said Mother she's beautiful. I could marry er.

Harriet E did did e?

Mrs Triggs   *He* could see it, even then! Now thun. Flowers for the ole lady.

Exit **Mrs Triggs**.

Maude   Some bugger better church William before I kill er.

Harriet   I would.

Maude   Kill er?

Harriet   Church William.

Maude   You hardly know im.

Harriet   I've seen enough.

Maude   E's desperate.

Harriet   I can tell.

Maude   Canya?

Harriet   Stinksa fish.

Enter **Bolitho**.
He carries his mother, wrapped head to foot in rugs.

Bolitho   Get a chair, put it by the slab there.

Harriet *finds a chair.*
Maude *assists* **Bolitho**.

Bolitho   She's stone cold. In this heat!

Maude   Sure she id'n dead?

Bolitho   She's breathin.

Maude   Feel er.

Harriet   Like ice.

They sit her in a chair and lean her against the slab.

Bolitho (*in her ear*)   'right Mother?!

Mother *nods her head.*

Maude   Mr Bolitho –

Bolitho Where's me dinner? What the hell is this?

Maude Injured Yorky.

Bolitho Off the table with im goddammit woman tis a kitchen not 'ospital tent! And that face is revolting (*Picking up a table cloth and passing it to* **Harriet**.) cover it up while I eat me dinner. I can't abide the sighta blood.

Maude *serves him his dinner.*

Bolitho Whass this? Tongue?

He sits and eats.

Maude Mr Bolitho –

Bolitho What is it Maude.

Maude Can I lay out Jumbo on a bed someplace? E's in a very bad way.

Bolitho Take im away. Anywhere you like.

Maude Thank you sir.

Maude *unwraps* **Jumbo** *and takes him off.*

Bolitho Chutney. Fetch me chutney.

Harriet *stays put.*

Bolitho Did you hear what I said?

Harriet Yes Mister.

Bolitho Then would you do as I ask?

Harriet No Mister.

Bolitho What?

Harriet Don't work ere Mister.

Bolitho Then what are you doin in my kitchen?

Harriet Come for a job Mister.

Bolitho Do you want a job?

Harriet Yes Mister.

Bolitho   Then fetch me the chutney.

Harriet   That a job?

Bolitho   What?

Harriet   If I fetch the chutney, mean I gotta job?

Bolitho   Yes. You have. It's called fetching the chutney.

Harriet   How much will you pay me?

Bolitho   What's it worth?

Harriet   Three pound Mister.

Bolitho   Three pound!

Harriet   Yes Mister.

Bolitho   To fetch the chutney?

Harriet   Thass a week.

Bolitho   How many times in a week are you gonna fetch the chutney for three pound?

Harriet   I'd do other tasks.

Bolitho   Why thank you. Such as what.

Harriet   Sweep the planchon Mister.

Bolitho   That's a start.

Harriet   You mean I gotta job?

Bolitho   What I mean is if you don't fetch the chutney you won't get a job.

Harriet *stays put.*

Bolitho   Now what?

Harriet   Where is the chutney Mister?

Bolitho   How the hell should I know? Try the larder.

Exit **Harriet** *to larder.*
Enter **Carne**, *a banker.*

Bolitho   Mr Carne. How's your bank.

Carne   Collapsed.

Bolitho   Much panic?

Carne   None whatever.

Bolitho (*yelling at scullery*)   Where's me chutney! (*To*
Carne.) Feel me mother willya? See what you make of er.

Carne *does as he's asked.*
Enter **Harriet**, *empty-handed.*

Bolitho   Now what?

Harriet   You want tomato chutney Mister? Apple chutney
Mister? Green bean Mister?

Bolitho   Will you stop callin me Mister!?

Harriet   Pumpkin –

Carne   She's cold.

Bolitho   Any ole chutney!

Exit **Harriet**.

Carne   Sure she's alive?

Bolitho   Reckon it's scarlet fever?

Carne   No sir. I can assure you that's not scarlet fever.
My father and brother recently died of it.

Bolitho   That's a relief.

Enter **Harriet** *with a jar of chutney.*

Bolitho   Bravo!

Harriet *dumps the chutney on the table.*

Bolitho (*to* **Carne**)   Name your price.

Carne   Well sir –

Bolitho   What?

Carne   I was hoping, bearing in mind the assets – the

properties in Penzance and Marazion, the shareholdings –

Bolitho   Yes?

Carne   That you might make –

Bolitho   An offer? Shillin.

Carne   That your offer?

Bolitho   Yes.

The fact that he is a ruined man hits **Carne** *at this moment.*
He starts to blub.
Bolitho *and* **Harriet** *watch, dispassionate.*

Carne (*at length, after making something of a recovery*)   I'm sorry
– I – forgive me – my brother died and then my father – I
lost em – we had such prospects for the new century – I'm
on my own – entirely alone – I was hoping –
compassion . . .

Bolitho   Have you brought the deeds? And forms of
assent?

Carne (*showing a thick sheaf of vellum*)   Here.

Bolitho   Take em through to the study. Third door down.
I shall sign em soon as I've ad me dinner.

Exit **Carne**.

I gave im sound advice twelvemonth back. E chose to
ignore it.

Harriet   You was too generous.

Bolitho   How d'ya mean?

Harriet   If you charged im e mighta took it.

Bolitho   What's your name?

Harriet   'arriet.

Bolitho   'arriet what?

Harriet   Screetch.

Bolitho   Where ya from 'arriet?

Harriet   Botallack.

Bolitho (*eating*)   Work at the mine?

Harriet   Till you shut it down.

Bolitho   I can't help that.

Harriet   Yes you can.

Bolitho   Eh?

Harriet   You 'eard.

Bolitho   Tin's below thirty-eight.

Harriet   So what?

Bolitho   You know as well as I do thass the critical price.

Harriet   I don't.

Bolitho   Well it is.

Harriet   Oo says?

Bolitho   You *want* this job?

Harriet   I dun't *want* the job Mister, I *need* the job cus
thanks to you me three brothers is emigrated. You know
em, Mister, Israel, Thomas and Gordon Screetch. You
offered to pay their passage. From Plymouth.

Plymouth docks.
African drums.
Harriet *hugs* **Israel** (**Billy**).
Gordon *and* **Thomas** *wait.*

Gordon   C'mon Israel.

Israel   C'mon 'arriet.

Thomas   Gangplank's goin up.

Hymn
  Speed them through the mighty ocean
  In the dark and stormy day

When the waves in wild commotion
Fill all others with dismay
Be thou with them
Drive their terrors far away . . .

Bolitho   Israel Screetch you say? Gordon? Thomas?

Gordon   'arriet, leave im go.

Harriet   I'll never see y'again!

Israel   Goodbye sister!

Thomas   We're only goin Bulawayo!

Hymn
When they reach the land of strangers
And the prospect dark appears
Nothing seen but toils and dangers,
Northing felt but doubts and fears
Be thou with them
Hear their sighs and bount their tears . . .

Bolitho   They turned my offer down.

Harriet   Exactly.

Bolitho   I can't elp that.

Israel   If e can douse out for we to go Africa e can
afford to keep the ruddy mine open!

African drums.
Enter **Tot**.

Scout (Tot)   There's four hundred natives on the banks of
the Donga!

Spreckly (Capps)   Are they hostile?

Scout   Bristling with projectiles!

Bolitho   Tot. Ave some dinner.

Tot   Both sides are amassin on Larrigan Bridge.

Bolitho (*to* **Harriet**)   Felt me mother?

Harriet Yes.

Bolitho Feel er again.

She does as she's told.

Tot There's Penzance boys and three score Yorkies on the east side and our buccas with Mousehole and Porthleven men to the west.

Harriet She's 'ot.

Bolitho (*rushing to his mother*) Hot?

Harriet Very 'ot.

Bolitho (*feeling her brow*) So she is.

Tot There's bound to be a battle.

Bolitho Shift er away from the slab 'arriet. Over there by the door.

Harriet *shifts* **Mother** *to where* **Jumbo** *was sat.*

Bolitho And get that thick rug off er.

Harriet *does as she's bid.*

Bolitho So my fine words buckled in the heat. I feared they might. Thank you Tot. I'll finish me dinner and get down there.

Tot I don't advise it.

Bolitho O?

Tot When they've finished with Penzance there's talk of findin you.

Bolitho Cover er with that.

He hands **Harriet** *the blanket that* **Jumbo** *was wrapped in.*

Harriet She's cooler already.

Bolitho (*assisting* **Harriet**) Wrap it round her head –

Tot Tack's none to appy with you. E don't like the way you've gone with the Yorkies on this.

Bolitho (*to* **Harriet**)   Go to the yard and pump up fresh cold water out the well.

Exit **Harriet**.

Tot   E's sayin you got both boots in the enemy camp.

Bolitho   Who the hell does Tack Bazely think e is? None too happy you say? With me. Bolitho! E dun't know what I'm doin. E think e know what I'm doin cus e pick up scraps like a dog but e don't know what I'm doin! E think I'm kowtowin to Capps! E's blind!

Tot   E's took control. E's in command.

Bolitho   Of what? The Army? The Navy? The country?

Tot   Our buccas.

Bolitho   The little shit!

Tot   I wouldn' set forth if I was you. In fact (*Looking round the kitchen.*) nowhere's safe.

Bolitho   I ad no choice with Capps.

Tot   I believe ya.

Bolitho   E forced me to listen.

Enter **Harriet** *with water.*

Bolitho   She was ere when e come round. (*to* **Harriet**.) Am I right? Eh?

Harriet   Oo?

Bolitho   Capps. I pleaded with the man Tot but e wouldn't budge would e? E demanded compensation. I ad to pay im. Now this ere, what's your name?

Harriet   'arriet.

Bolitho   'arriet what?

Harriet   Screetch.

Bolitho   What?

Harriet Screetch!

Bolitho She's born witness to that and she's no damned businessman or magistrate's clerk or p'lice inspector she's a what are ya?

Harriet Stone-breaker.

Bolitho Up Botallack.

Harriet Till you shut it down.

Bolitho All right! So Tot, you go back and tell that slippery little bastard Tack Bazely to come ere and face me and make his accusations.

Exit **Tot**.

Harriet I arn't witness to nothin.

Bolitho Eh?

Harriet You paid the man six undred pound.

Bolitho Yes.

Harriet But I dunno why you did it.

Bolitho For the good of the port.

Harriet Why not shut it down?

Bolitho What?

Harriet You shut down Botallack –

Bolitho I ad to.

Harriet With six undred pound in your pocket?

Bolitho It don't work like that.

Harriet Yes it do.

Bolitho Don't argue –

Harriet You spent six undred pound for the people of this port. How come you couldn't spend it on the poor buggers up Botallack? Insteada shippin em off to Africa? What's so ruddy different about Botallack?

Bolitho   I've wasted thousands on Botallack.

Harriet   Wasted?

Bolitho   Yes. Thousands.

Harriet   How many ya made?

Bolitho   I've poured cartloads down that shaft, 'arriet. Tis what we call in business a dead loss. The harbour is a goin concern. With the North Pier it got the capacity but we have to keep the trade. Understand? Dead loss. That's what we call it.

Harriet   Like matey's bank.

Bolitho   Bank's different again. E got debts beyond the value of 'is assets. So I'm purchasing the bank plus the debt. I coulda gived im a loan. If 'is brother was alive I woulda done but this man's not capable. The long and the short of it is in business terms the wrong brother died.

Harriet *takes the guilder from her pocket and places it on the table in front of* **Bolitho**.

Bolitho   Hell's this?

Harriet   For the bank.

Bolitho   What is it?

Harriet   African shillin.

Bolitho   I gotta shilling of my own thank you.

Harriet   Thass for me to buy the bank.

Bolitho   Do you ave the capital to realise 'is debts?

Harriet (*mumbles*)   Nnope.

Bolitho   Speak up.

Harriet   No!

Bolitho   I got the capital see? I got interest. Pilchards, smelters, tannery, broccoli, property, shippin. That's how I can afford to buy a bank for a shillin.

Harriet (*toying with the coin*)   Israel sent me that.

Bolitho   Did e now.

Harriet   E won't be sendin any more cus Israel's dead.

Bolitho   Sorry to 'ear it.

Harriet   You killed im.

Bolitho   O did I.

Harriet   Yes.

Bolitho   If I ad'n shut the mine down Israel wouldna gone to where was it?

Harriet   Bulawayo.

Bolitho   And now e'd be alive and kickin.

Harriet   Thass about the size of it.

Bolitho (*eating*)   Check me mother.

Harriet *inspects* **Mother**.

Bolitho (*eating*)   First Tack now you. Risin above your ruddy station. Pronouncing on what you know bugger all about.

Harriet   She need air.

Bolitho   You reckon?

Harriet   Can't breathe can ya Mother.

Bolitho   Wanna go out dear?

Harriet   Sit er in the shade.

Bolitho   Under the oak for an hour?

Harriet   In the breeze.

Bolitho   This chutney's disgustin.

Harriet   Tis pumpkin.

Bolitho   I asked for tomata.

Harriet   No ya didn.

Bolitho   There ya go again!

Harriet   You said any ole chutney.

Bolitho   Don't like pumpkin.

Harriet   Shoulda told me.

Bolitho   Every bugger knows. There's not a domestic in the whole damn district oo don't know I don't like pumpkin.

Harriet   I don't.

Bolitho   Bring me tomata!

Harriet   Fetch it yourself.

Bolitho   Goddammit.

Harriet   I arn't budgin.

Bolitho   This is no way to greet the nineteen 'undreds. No way at all.

Exit **Bolitho** *to scullery.*
Enter **Mrs Triggs** *with a bunch of flowers, followed by* **Rundle**, *a gardener.*
Mrs Triggs *puts the flowers into the pitcher.*

Mrs Triggs (*indicates* **Mother**)   This man's a Yorky.

Rundle   Is e by godfathers.

Mrs Triggs   And the bugger's bin courtin one a my domestics.

Rundle   We can't have that.

Mrs Triggs   Then put im in 'andcart, run im down arbour and dump im on a Yorky boat. (*Gathering up the tobacco.*) And e can 'ave is damned tobacca back.

Harriet   Er . . .

Mrs Triggs (*picking up flowers*)   There now. Id'n that a picture? Nothin like the scenta daffodils when you're dyin.

Exit **Mrs Triggs** *with flowers*.

Rundle (*on closer inspection*) Thass no Yorky.

Harriet No.

Enter **Bolitho** *with tomato chutney*.

Bolitho (*sitting at table*) Rundle. Take me mother out and sit er under the oak.

Rundle Under the oak.

Bolitho In the breeze.

Exit **Rundle** *with* **Mother**.
Bolitho *sits and eats his dinner*.
Enter **Borlase**, *breathless*.

Bolitho Borlase. Want some dinner?

Borlase I fear I shall never eat again.

Bolitho What's the matter with you man?

Borlase Please! Don't ask me nothing more!

Bolitho Borlase –

Borlase I have seen such a sight as I never wished to see – a thousand fiends of hell, bent on destruction!

Bolitho Sit down and tell us all about it.

Borlase Penzance is boiling with wrath!

Hymn
God save our native land
May his protective hand
Still guard our shore.
May peace her power extend
Foe be transformed to friend
And Britain's rights depend
On war no more . . .

Bolitho Now thun Borlase.

Borlase I did your bidding, I went to Penzance, cleared

the upline, hired packers and prepared the quay for
Uttings, Thirkles and Capps. The first Yorky boat tied up
and landed. I then embarked on my return journey. The
place was seething. Police recruiting specials have took on
every thug and vagabond known to the bench! I was
caught up in the crowd. I couldn't turn back. They was
headed for Larrigan Bridge. Hundreds of em, all familiar
faces – arsonists, pederasts, rapists, bidding me good day,
smiling at me, assuming I was one of them! We reached
the bridge, the crowd was fourteen thick and surging
forward, I was crushed. The stench of alcohol and
perspiration! In this weather! In the distance on the far side
I could make out the bobbing heads of our buccas straining
to join with the enemy. One man stood between them,
held the bridge against the Penzance mob. Johnny Torse, a
fisherman of French extraction well known to the bench.

Bolitho   Big chap.

Borlase   Huge!

Bolitho   Thickset.

Borlase   Chest like a barrel.

Harriet   Strong.

Bolitho   Married a Richards.

Borlase   Did e.

Harriet   E can pick up orse.

Bolitho   Can e 'arriet.

Harriet   Small orse. Seen im do it. Up Botallack.

Bolitho   Alive or dead?

Harriet   Dead. Thass eavier. Dead's eavier.

Borlase   He bestrode the bridge with a metal plate held
before him.

Torso *standing on bridge, as described.*

Bolitho   The Penzance mob started dobbing stones and

rocks which glanced and struck the iron shield like bells!
He was yelling at us in Gallic this Goliath –

Torso *yells obscenities in French.*

Borlase   There was nothin they could do to shift im.
Boulders, missiles, rocks, e was impervious to em all. And
our buccas, I could see em, cheering ever louder till
clamour rose to roar but Torso, they call im that, turning
to acknowledge the crowd's adulation exposed his back to
the Penzance onslaught. The chimes and rings of stone on
iron turned to thuds as quartz and granite rained upon his
broad, bronzed, naked shoulders. The man next to me,
Abel Kent, a demon with the cricket ball, took careful aim
and hurled a fist-sized lump of spar which connected with
the back of Torso's skull with such a force and thud that
for a brief moment both armies froze, silent. Torso swayed
back, forth, back, forth and fell forward with a clang!

Torso *falls forward.*

Borlase   Stillness turned to mayhem in a trice. Both sides
surged and rushed upon the other, trampling the forgotten
giant. I was literally picked up off my feet and carried
forward by the mob. The advance towards our buccas was
relentless. The stench of violence filled my nostrils.
Taunting yells turned to grunts as Penzance engaged its
sworn enemy, our buccas! Before me's nothing but fists,
staves, batons, bent bodies and . . .

Harriet   Blood!

Borlase   The battle spread to a brawl and brawl to rout.

Bolitho   Who won?

Borlase   Penzance sir.

Bolitho   Penzance.

Borlase   Our buccas was humiliated. Defeat has done
nothin to quell their rage.

Enter **Tot**.

Tot   There's gangs of men hunting down scapegoats. Property's at risk.

Bolitho   Is there no sign of the Army?

Tot   Just left Redruth.

Bolitho   Thass twenty ruddy miles up the line!

Tot   We want the Riot Act. Us older ones.

Bolitho   Borlase –

Borlase   No!

Bolitho   For Chrissake man.

Borlase   Not the Riot Act.

Bolitho   Listen.

Borlase   Don't send me off again.

Bolitho   Go to me study.

Borlase   I've suffered quite enough for a man of my disposition.

Bolitho   My study!

Borlase   Ah.

Bolitho   Look in the top left-hand drawer of the rolltop desk for my copy of the Riot Act.

Borlase   Please, don't ask me to go and read it!

Bolitho   I'm tellin you to fetch it. Thass all.

Borlase   Thank you sir.

Bolitho   Then you can go ome.

Borlase   Much obliged.

Bolitho   Thank Mr Carne the banker for 'is patience and tell im if I ever finish me dinner I shall be in there to sign his documentation.

Exit **Borlase**.

Enter **Mrs Triggs**, *carrying flowers*.

Mrs Triggs Mr Bolitho! (*Transfixed by* **Mother***'s empty chair*.) O! Sir! I'm so dreadfully dreadfully sorry! (*Falling at his feet*.) Forgive me I've done a ghastly ghastly thing!

Enter **Maude**.

Maude Bloody woman!

Mrs Triggs I've made an awesome mistake.

Maude I've ad enough.

Mrs Triggs Tis a resignation matter.

Maude It's er or me!

Mrs Triggs If you want me to go I shall walk out that door.

Bolitho What the hell is goin on?

Maude She walked in the room, took one look at Jumbo and screamed.

Bolitho What have you done woman?

Maude I can go with who I like!

Mrs Triggs I can't bring meself to say it!

Bolitho Say what?

Mrs Triggs You should never a took me on all those years ago cus if you ad'n this wouldn't have appened.

Bolitho Godsake woman, tell me what ya done!

Mrs Triggs Never hire staff outa compassion.

Bolitho Aw for Chrissake.

Mrs Triggs When I turned up after me husband drowned starvin with little William beggin for work you shoulda slammed the door in me face.

Bolitho Wish to God I ad.

Mrs Triggs Every single domestic oo's took a situation

ere's come in off the mines. They're not suited to indoor
work. They're uncouth clumsy and crude but you can't
sack em. How many have I brung ere, twenty-eight? And
what's our capacity?

Bolitho   Willya stop ramblin?

Mrs Triggs   You're payin scores thousands for doin
bugger all.

Harriet   Eh?

Maude   She's right.

Bolitho   I don't need you to tell me that!

Mrs Triggs   Then sack us!

Harriet   Scores? Thousands? Bugger all?

Maude   We deserve it don't you think?

Mrs Triggs   Poor distressed creatures that we are.

Harriet (*heading for the door*)   Distressed? Creatures?

Mrs Triggs   Throw us out in the fields to starve!

Bolitho   Harriet!

Harriet (*on her way out*)   I don't go beggin for work –

Bolitho (*to* **Mrs Triggs**)   Now look what ya done.

Harriet   I don't want charity Uncle.

Maude   Then get out!

Harriet   I'm goin.

Bolitho   Come back.

Maude   At last. Somebody you can sack!

Harriet   I never took the job in the first place.

Bolitho   Do you want one?

Harriet (*at door*)   I'm too good to work for a cake like
you!

Mrs Triggs   Don't be so damn proud!

Harriet   And you can stuff the duchess up your ass!

Mrs Triggs   What?!

Maude   Pride never paid for butcher's meat!

Harriet   You go wi' Yorkies for yours.

Maude (*picking up a knife*)   Take that back.

Harriet   No.

Maude   Take it back.

Bolitho   Put it down!

Harriet   No!

Maude   No!

Bolitho   Take it back!

Harriet   Put it down!

Maude *stabs* **Harriet**.
Harriet *screams and collapses*.
Maude *throws down the knife*.
Exit **Maude**.

Bolitho   Maude!
Bolitho *picks the knife up*.
It stays in his hand.

Mrs Triggs (*to* **Harriet**)   You deserved it. Sayin that about a duchess!

Mrs Triggs *makes for the door*.

Bolitho   Where ya goin?

Mrs Triggs   Fetch your mother back.

Bolitho   Where's she gone?

Mrs Triggs   I ordered Rundle take er down 'arbour and stick er on the deck of a Yorky steam drifter with several pounds of cheap tobacca!

Exit **Mrs Triggs**.

Bolitho   Eh? Mother? But –

Harriet (*alone*)   Help!

Bolitho   Patience 'arriet! Mrs Triggs!

Exit **Bolitho**.
Enter **Mother**.
She stands, pipe in mouth, swathed in a cloud of smoke.

Mother   I've ad me breath of air and a chuff on some Black. I'm ready for me breakfast now.

She sits at the table, smoking.
Enter **Borlase**.
He's semi-catatonic.
Enter **Bolitho**.

Bolitho   Borlase. Run after Mrs . . . Mother!

Borlase   Mr Carne has hanged himself.

Harriet   Help.

Bolitho   Hanged himself?

Borlase   I don't have the stomach to cut him down.

Bolitho   Carne? In my study?

Borlase   Off the butcher's ook in the beam above the rolltop desk.

He hands **Bolitho** *a piece of paper.*

Bolitho   What's this?

Borlase   Riot Act.

Bolitho   Ad e . . . did e sign the documentation?

Borlase   I can't say I noticed.

Mother   I want me breakfast.

Bolitho   Mother willya wait?

Harriet   Help.

Bolitho You too 'arriet. Borlase . . .

Borlase Don't ask me! No more. I thought the study would be safe.

Bolitho Tis best to do something Borlase. The damn fool's hanged himself, you can't bring im back and you're a lucky man because you are alive and there's much to be done. We need somebody to cut im down and medication for the girl.

Mother Breakfast.

Bolitho Now Borlase. A simple task. (*Indicating cupboard.*) Go to the cupboard and fetch the medication.

Borlase, *in a trance, does as he's told.*

Mother Oo's that?

Bolitho Borlase.

Mother Izze frisky?

Bolitho No Mother e's in want of medication.

Mother Thass no good to me.

Harriet Help . . .

Bolitho (*attending to* **Harriet**) Tis all right dear. (*Turning away.*) Aw Christ look at the blood. Great clots of it! Hold your hand tight on the wound.

Borlase (*panicked*) There's none there! Cupboard's empty!

Enter **Maude**, *with medication.*

Maude I ad to take the bandages off Jumbo.

Bolitho Maude!

Maude (*preparing medication*) Where did I get ya?

Mother Breakfast!

Bolitho Borlase, boil me mother an egg.

Harriet In the chest.

Bolitho How deep?

Harriet Damn deep.

Maude Don't look.

Bolitho I can't abear the sight of blood.

Harriet Am I dead?

Bolitho No! Don't think of it.

Harriet Tis bleedin.

Bolitho Blood's nothin.

Harriet Tis best kept on the inside don't you think?

Enter **Tot**.

Tot Army's reached St Erth.

Bolitho Thanks Tot.

Tot Whass up with er?

Bolitho Bin stabbed. Foller me Tot.

Tot (*suspicious of* **Bolitho***'s knife*) Where to?

Bolitho My study. I gotta pick up me Lord Lieutenant
regalia for to meet the Army off the train. While we're in
there we shall cut down Carne the banker off the butcher's
ook above the rolltop and check that documentation.

Tot Carne?

Bolitho Yes e's dead too. No more questions Tot.

Exit **Bolitho** *and* **Tot**.

Harriet Me brother got a spear through 'is neck.

Maude Did e.

Harriet His throat was like a gutted cod.

Maude So you come off light.

African drums.

Spreckly Henceforth the possession of weapons is a capital offence! The Tribal Elders have been notified that if a British Army Patrol spies a Matabele warrior armed with a spear, he will be summarily shot!

Maude *kneels beside* **Harriet** *with swabs, liniment, etc.*

Harriet (*exposing her wound*) Ere –

Maude (*recoiling*) Chutney?!

Harriet Sh!

Mother Where's me breakfast?

Enter **Bolitho**.
He carries a ceremonial chain, the knife and **Carne***'s documents.*

Bolitho Tot's layin out Carne on the chaise and coverin im with the Persian rug. The bugger'd signed so that's all right. I'm off to meet the Army. Whilst I'm down there I shall arrange for a doctor and an undertaker. How's 'arriet?

Maude Tis hellish deep.

Bolitho Did she puncture an organ?

Maude Heart I think.

Bolitho Heart!

Harriet 'avin trouble beatin.

Enter **Matthews** *and* **Billy**, *manacled.*

Matthews Got the bugger.

Bolitho Charged im?

Matthews O yes!

Bolitho What with.

Matthews Assault and battery (*Tipping the knives out of the sack.*), possession of lethal weapons –

Bolitho Theft of cutlery.

Billy That's a lie!

Mother   Oo's that?

Bolitho   Billy Triggs Mother.

Mother   Is e frisky?

Bolitho   E's in irons.

Mother   Thass no good to me.

Bolitho   I'm deeply disillusioned with you Billy. What is it's transformed you into this . . . this criminal?

Billy   I'm innocent.

Bolitho   I've 'eard they words a thousand times on the bench and every time I give the same reply. If you choose the path of crime for whatever reason and walk down the path of crime you must be prepared to go all the way down the path of crime to the gallows if necessary.

Harriet   No!

Billy   'arriet?!

Harriet   Israel!

African drums.

Israel   I've bin Levant Mine there's no work there, Gordon's bin Camborne tried Wheal Busy, Ding Dong, Dolcoath, there's men laid off all over the county so me and the boys 'ave booked a passage to Africa.

Harriet   Africa?

Israel   Bulawayo! We'll send you money back 'arriet. Lucky money. Guilders!

Harriet (*weakly*)   Bin stabbed.

Billy   Stabbed?

Matthews   Stabbed! Who stabbed ya?

Harriet (*pointing at* **Bolitho**)   E did.

Bolitho   Me!

Harriet   Yes.

Billy   Bolitho?

Matthews   Stabbed ya?

Harriet   Yes!

Bolitho (*dropping the knife*)   No!

Harriet   Through the heart –

Billy (*to* **Matthews**)   Arrest im!

Bolitho (*pointing at* **Maude**)   She did it!

Maude   Me?

Bolitho   Maude.

Billy   Maude?

Maude   I'm nursin er.

Bolitho   'arriet. It's one thing to say I killed your brother. It's quite another to accuse me of murderin you.

Matthews (*suspicious*)   Her brother?

Bolitho   Borlase!

Borlase (*dropping a tray full of assorted kitchen objects assembled for* **Mother***'s breakfast*)   No! Don't blame me! I didn't do it! Please! No more!

Exit **Borlase**, *running.*

Bolitho   Dammit e coulda told ya. Where's Mrs Triggs? She was ere, find er!

Enter **Tot**.

Bolitho   Tot!

Tot   The body's laid out on the chaise longue. I covered it with the Persian rug.

Matthews   Body? What body?

Billy   Er brother.

Tot   Carne the banker.

Matthews   Another one?

Billy   Where?

Tot   In 'is study. Ugly ole death.

Matthews   Carne too?

Bolitho   I'm bein wrongly accused ere Tot, will ya track down Mrs Triggs for me?

Tot   She alive or dead?

Bolitho   Alive!

Tot   Where's she to?

Bolitho   Gone to get me mother.

Tot   Your mother's ere.

Mother   Oo's that?

Bolitho   Tot Tonkin Mother! She's down 'arbour Tot.

Mother   Is e frisky?

Bolitho   E's goin after Mrs Triggs!

Mother   Thass no good to me.

Bolitho (*to* **Tot**)   Ask Geoffrey Budd the undertaker to come up ere will ya? Don't tell'n oo it's for cus I don't want the nature of Carne's death spread all over town.

Mother   Breakfast!

Bolitho   And tell the Army to stay aboard the train till I get there for the official welcome and photograph. And find Borlase –

Harriet   Doctor!

Bolitho   O yes. Doctor for 'arriet Tot.

Exit **Tot**.

Matthews   Just what exactly is the nature of Carne's death Mr Bolitho?

Harriet   E killed im and all.

Bolitho   'anged 'imself.

Harriet   Buyin 'is bank for a shillin.

Bolitho   'arriet!

A window breaks and a rock lands at **Bolitho***'s feet.* **Bolitho**
walks to the window.
Enter **Tot**.

Tot   Place is surrounded by buccas. Shrubbery's crawlin
with em. And they're lookin mean.

Bolitho *goes to the window.*

Bolitho   One a my domestics out there? Whippin em up?

Billy   Sarah.

Tot   She's wild.

Billy   She'll stop at nothin.

Tot   Er and Tack Bazely.

Matthews   I ah . . .

Bolitho   Stay ere Matthews.

Matthews   Was thinkin of gettin 'elp.

Bolitho   Who?

Matthews   Jack Tamblyn?

Bolitho   His leg's in irons. Take im a day to get ere.

Tot   There's talk of a lynching.

Bolitho (*stroking his neck*)   Thanks Tot.

Exit **Tot**.
Another window is smashed.
Outside, the indecipherable rantings of **Sarah** *and* **Tack***, plus the
occasional muffled response.*

Bolitho   Release 'im Matthews.

Matthews   Sir?

Another window smashed.

Bolitho   Free Triggs!

Matthews   But –

Bolitho   Do it!

Matthews (*mumbling as he unmanacles* **Billy**)   Capture
Triggs e says. Bin chasin the bastard all day. Climbed
Clifton 'ill four times! Down Jack Lane, 'cross the Strand,
up the Fradgeon, back down Chapel, over Gwavas, St
Peters, Adit Lane, Chywoon, Treneglos, Ice Plant, id'n a
street in all the port I ab'm chased'n up'n down less'n
twice. I catch the bugger bring im ere and now I'm told to
let im go!

Mother   Oo's that?

Bolitho   Inspector Matthews Mother!

Mother   Is e frisky?

Bolitho   Mother take some rest willya? Maude lay er out
and stroke er brow, put er to sleep.

Maude *does as she's asked.*
Billy *is free.*

Sarah (*off*)   Come out Bolitha!

Enter **Borlase**.

Borlase   There's buccas everywhere out there. Wounded
tigers every one. I was pounced on. Bin sent to get you.

Bolitho (*offering his hands to* **Matthews**)   Arrest me.

Matthews   What's the charge?

Bolitho   Murder.

Matthews   You're confessin?

Bolitho   Yes. I slaughtered Carne, killed er brother and
'ad a stab at 'er.

Matthews *manacles him.*

Borlase   What?!

Bolitho   No buts Borlase. Go and tell em I'm under
arrest.

Tack (*off*)   Borlase!

Borlase   You sure about this?

Bolitho   I know what these domestics are capable of.
Custody's the only protection I've got. A charge of multiple
homicide, the prospect of a humiliating journey through the
courts follered by public execution in Bodmin should take
the sting out their tail don't you think, and send the buccas
'ome content?

Borlase   You can only 'ope.

Exit **Borlase**.

Hymn
  O God our help in ages past
  Our hope for years to come,
  Be thou our guard while life shall last,
  And our eternal home.

  Time, like an ever-rolling stream,
  Bears all its sons away,
  They fly forgotten, as a dream
  Dies at the dawn of day.

Spoken over hymn:

Bolitho   Now thun Billy. What y' gonna do? Lynch me
or help me out?

Billy   Mister, I bin sayin all along no violence. Last night,
when I saw y'outside the chapel I was urgin buccas then to
keep it peaceful. Tot will bear me out on that. Dawn we
boarded the Yorky boats all quiet as you please, singin'
'ymns! They stood back and let us do the job and went
and ad their breakfast. Then e started chasing me. You

ordered Strick to divert Yorky boats to Penzance and
events got outa control. There was nothin I could do to
stop it cus everywhere I turned there was the copper.
Crowds of sad defeated men, battered and cowed by
Penzance are lookin for someone to blame. They want
blood. Are you surprised they've come up ere? Cus if you
are you're out of touch Uncle with the very port and
people you claim to love. But do you love em Mr Bolitho?
You've murdered two and stabbed another! And if you
choose the path of crime for whatever reason and walk
down it you must be prepared to go all the way, to the
gallows of neccesary!

Enter **Borlase**, *running*

Borlase They're in no mood to listen Bolitha! Prepare
yourself! For the worst!

Bolitho Matthews get out there and read the Riot Act.

Exit **Matthews** *with Riot Act.*

Borlase Heathen! Animals!

Bolitho Borlase!

Enter **Tack** *and* **Sarah**, *with rope.*
Exit **Borlase**, *running.*

Sarah There e is!

Tack Lynch the bastard!

Harriet E stabbed me!

Billy Look at this e's knifed er!

Sarah Stuck er through!

Sarah *runs around half-crazed, setting up the rope for a lynching.*
African drumming.
Bulawayo.
A Matabele Warrior (**Bolitho**) *is arraigned before* **Spreckly**.

Spreckly On Saturday last you launched a spear at
Israel Screetch who for the price of a meagre shilling which
he sent home to his beloved sister, forsook his Saturday

cricket to protect the interests of the Crown. You got the little bugger through the neck! I sentence you with the power invested in me by Her Imperial Majesty Queen Victoria, Empress of India, to death by firing squad. Do you have anything to say in mitigation?

Bolitho *stands on the floor with the noose around his neck.* **Sarah** *has hold of the other end of the rope, which is run through a block attached to a butcher's hook in the beam.* **Sarah** *stands on the table ready to jump, and lynch* **Bolitho**.

Matthews This is mob rule! He's entitled to a fair trial! Cut him down!

Bolitho God's sake Matthews if y'can't stop em let em get on with it. I got nothin to fear. I'm an honourable man. I did everything for the sake of the port and its people. If this is all the thanks I get then speed me to eternity and bollocks to the nineteen undreds. They can kiss me ass. Do your worst and make it quick. Aw, wait. Is me mother asleep yet Maude?

Maude Just gone off.

Bolitho Leave er slumber. Tell er I said goodbye.

Spreckly Load! Aim!

Sarah *bends to the rope.*

Harriet Ceasefire.

Spreckly What?!

Harriet Ceasefire!

Bolitho Quiet 'arriet!

Sarah Git on with it!

Harriet Stop!

Bolitho Take no notice of er, she's ramblin.

Harriet The bank!

Bolitho I've told you before 'arriet you can't 'ave it.

Sarah   What bank?

Bolitho   Tis nothin, she wanna buy a bank, thass all.

Spreckly   Take im!

Tack   'old 'ard!

Harriet   Ceasefire!

Spreckly   As you were.

Tack   Which bank?

Bolitho   Carne's bank went bust today.

Tack   Aw yeah we knaw about that.

Sarah   Right this is it!

Spreckly   Take aim!

Billy   'old on –

Harriet   Ceasefire!

Sarah   Whassamatter now!

Billy   You said she wanted to buy it?

Bolitho   It's too late she's more dead than I am.

Billy   Oo's she gonna buy the bank off if Carne is dead?

Sarah   'oo owns this bank?

Bolitho   He came up ere and tried to salvage it but I refused a loan, businessman that I am, and I bought it off im for a shillin.

Sarah   A shillin?

Bolitho   That do ya? Now!

Billy   Why did you kill im?

Bolitho   I didn't kill im! The bugger 'anged imself. E's in me study if you care to look with a noose around 'is neck. Third door down on the left.

Billy   So you didn't kill im.

Harriet Yes e did.

Bolitho Go and see for yourself.

Sarah *hops off the table.*
Exit **Sarah**.

Harriet (*very weak*) Think I'm dyin.

Bolitho 'arriet. I know you blame me for sendin your brothers off to Africa. That's the way it is in business. When prosperity reigns do we get thanked? No. We got the nineteen undreds –

Billy Which brothers?

Bolitho Israel Thomas and Gordon Screetch. When we shut Botallack they went to Bulawayo. Israel died . . .

Billy Where?

Bolitho Bulawayo!

Billy You killed im?

Bolitho Yes!

Enter **Sarah**.

Sarah Carne's under the Persian rug. I swep' that bugger this mornin.

Billy How did e die?

Sarah (*hopping on to the table and taking the rope*) 'anged imself all right.

Bolitho See?

Billy E didn't murder the brother neither.

Sarah (*bending to the rope*) E stabbed a domestic, thass enough for me.

Harriet I'm fadin! Let me buy the bank, please, and pass it on to me brothers. Them that's still alive.

Billy That sound reasonable.

Sarah   All right, sell er the bank then we'll 'ang ya.

Tack   Fair enough?

Bolitho   I've told er. No. It would be an act of pure sentiment and you cannot allow sentiment to intercede in business. It's weak. Look at Carne. E was weak. E cried and then e killed imself. That is pathetic. You can't bow to that! Sorry, 'arriet, no bank. Thass final. Sarah do your business.

Spreckly   Ready! Aim!

Matthews   Wait!

Spreckly   Stop!

Sarah   Right! Thass the last time!

Matthews   This man has not committed a capital offence.

Harriet   Yes e ave e killed me brother killed im sure as 'ell.

Bolitho   They gotta theory up Botallack Matthews if a man pissed e caused the flood.

Billy   E stabbed 'arriet.

Matthews   That is a serious crime but you can't hang him for that.

Harriet   Gotta die ave I to get justice?

Bolitho   Yes 'arriet, thass the way it's lookin

Harriet *dies*.

Billy   'arriet?

Maude *attends* **Harriet**.

Maude   She's dead.

Tack (*to* **Matthews**)   That do ya?

Bolitho   Dead?

Spreckly   Ready!

Billy   Dead! Look at er. Face like an angel. Why did you kill er Bolitha? Why did you stab this sweet virtuous little maid!

Bolitho   Sweet? Virtuous?

Matthews   You're in trouble now Bolitho.

Spreckly   Aim!

Billy   Me mother always said you was a murderous bastard.

Bolitho   Eh?

Mrs Triggs   E's a cold, sinister man.

Sarah   Right! I'm gonna jump!

Bolitho   Wait!

Sarah   No thass it cap'm I'm jumpin.

Bolitho (*commanding*)   Sarah do as you're told for once!

Sarah *waits.*

Bolitho   Your mother? Mrs Triggs?

Mrs Triggs   Gotta killer's soul.

Bolitho   A killer's . . .

Spreckly   Fire!

African drums.
The first shot is fired by **Mrs Triggs**.

Bolitho (*clutching his chest*)   Mean to tell me after all those years of comin into my house every day, talking to me, working, cookin, cleanin, fawning at my guests, she thinks that of me? Nobody knows me better than Mrs Triggs.

Matthews   Must say I've ad me doubts.

Bolitho   Have you Matthews? You see another side of me on the bench of course, you and Borlase.

Matthews   Borlase! Hah! He hates your guts!

Borlase   Mean, scheming, heard-hearted bastard.

Bolitho   Borlase?

Spreckly   Fire!

Borlase *fires.*
Bolitho *clutches his stomach.*

Bolitho   Who else?

Maude (*after looking round*)   Me.

Bolitho   You, Maude?

Maude   None of us domestics much like ya, do us, Sarah.

Sarah   I've bin lookin forward to this since the day I got ere.

Spreckly   Fire!

Bolitho *gets it in the balls.*

Tack   'arbour master.

Bolitho   Strick?

Billy   E can't abide ya.

Tack   Pengelly boys . . .

Billy   Blewitts.

Tack   Richards clan.

Bolitho   The fishermen of this port? O no no no no that can't be right.

Spreckly   At random! Fire!

A volley of shots makes **Bolitho** *dance and jerk like a puppet.*

Bolitho (*broken*)   I'm a good man, arn't I?

No response..

Billy?

Billy   I arn't so sure Mr Bolitha. I used to think you was, but . . .

Bolitho Look at 'er. (*Standing over* **Harriet**, *looking down*.) D'you think I don't regret her death?

Sarah Easy to say, innit. With a noose around your neck.

Bolitho I can't die like this. I'm a good man. O 'arriet, before today I didn't know ya and here I am weeping over your dead damn body. If I could bring you back to life. If I could pump one more breath of air into your empty lungs and lift the lids off sightless eyes I would, I would say yes, have the ruddy bank!

Maude You would?

Bolitho Yes, yes, a thousand times yes.

The distant sound of a train's whistle.

Billy The Army!

Sarah Bollocks!

Tack Jump!

Sarah jumps.
The noose tightens.
Harriet *stands up.*
As she rises she lifts **Bolitho** *on her shoulders.*
Sarah *drops the rope.*

Bolitho ?

Harriet *scrapes a handful of 'blood' off her dress and holds it up under* **Bolitho**'s *nose.*

Bolitho Chutney! You little bitch!

Sarah (*going*) C'on Tack!

Tack (*going*) C'on Bill!

Exit **Tack** *and* **Sarah**.

Harriet (*grabbing* **Billy** *on his way out*) I wanna talk to you.

Bolitho Get me outa this Matthews.

Matthews *unmanacles* **Bolitho**.

Harriet   Sweet? Virtuous? Face of an angel?

Billy   Well . . .

Harriet   Mean to say you didn't mean it?

Billy   You was dead at the time.

Maude (*taking the bandages off* **Harriet**)   Prefer em dead do ya?

Bolitho (*the noose still round his neck*)   Maude!

Maude   Sir?

Bolitho   You're fired.

Maude   Eh?

Bolitho   You 'eard. Go upstairs, pick your damned Yorky up and get outa here. You too Screetch.

Harriet   'bout the bank?

Bolitho   Bugger the bank. And take Billy with ya.

Billy   Mr Bolitho –

Bolitho   No buts Billy, bugger off.

Enter **Borlase**.

Borlase   Army's reached Long Rock. I can't begin to describe the relief!

Bolitho *steps out of his noose and into his chain.*

Bolitho   Well, don't bother cus you're fired.

Borlase (*terrified*)   What?

Bolitho   Mean scheming heard-hearted bastard, am I?

Enter **Capps**.

Capps   Bolitho!

Bolitho   Not now, Capps.

Capps I want a word with you.

Bolitho The Army's ere what more d'ya want?

Capps Justice. (*Points at* **Billy**.) I want to see him and his confederates in the dock.

Borlase (*barging in front of* **Capps**) Excuse me. Now look ere Bolitho. I've bin through hell and high water for you. Down Wherrytown, across the bridge, along the prom, I've dodged stones, bayonets, barrel staves, several times bin recognised, mistaken for a thug and come face to face with a cadaver! These are duties beyond the calling of a magistrate's clerk but did I grumble? No! Did I shirk? No! And what thanks do I get? Dismissal! That's not fair Mr Bolitho.

Bolitho (*to* **Capps**) Tomorrow mornin. Ten o'clock. Town 'all. Preliminary hearings. That suit ya?

Capps For now.

Borlase E ignored every bloody thing I said.

Bolitho Mr Borlase will preside.

Borlase What?

Bolitho You know what to do.

Borlase Me?

Bolitho Magistrate.

Borlase Me?

Bolitho Yes Borlase.

Capps They're hissing at me!

Borlase Silence, Mr Capps!

Capps Your honour! I'm being hissed at!

Borlase You! Squincher! Stop hissing at Mr Capps or I shall clear the court!

Squincher F'kin stop me 'issin Mister!

Capps Arrest him for contempt!

Squincher Chuck me out I'll 'iss all down the f'kin street.

Capps I demand protection!

Squincher E's the f'ker f'kin started all this!

Borlase Thass enough Squincher!

Squincher Put e in the f'kin dock I'll quit 'issin!

Capps Arrest im for contempt!

Borlase E *is* arrested.

Squincher F'kin come ere, I'm still f'kin fightable!

Borlase Call Mr William Triggs to the witness-box.

Capps He can't give evidence!

Squincher Yes e f'kin can!

Capps He's standing in the dock!

Borlase Mr Capps –

Capps – he's a defendant!

The accused start to sing:

Hymn
The foe behind, the deep before,
Our hosts have dared and passed the sea.
And Pharoah's warriors strew the shore,
And Israel's ransomed tribes are free . . .

Capps This is a travesty! Hymns? You can't sing in court!

Borlase Stop hissin!

Squincher When I stop f'kin 'issin I d'start 'ittin.

Hymn
Happy morrow,
Turning sorrow,

Into peace and mirth!
Bondage ending,
Love descending,
O'er the earth!

Tack Kick out the Queen!

Borlase Silence!

Sarah (*a knife in her hand, her mouth dripping with blood*) Come ere Borlase I wanna slit your throat!

Borlase (*clutching his neck*) No!

Tack Call Carne the banker!

Carne *swings back and forth in front of* **Borlase** *like a pendulum.*

Borlase Put im back!

Bolitho Borlase?

Borlase All charges are dropped!

Capps I'm off to Plymouth!

Exit **Capps**.

Bolitho Borlase!

Borlase Uh!

Bolitho Make your mind up?

Borlase Er . . .

Bolitho What's it to be?

Borlase I'm 'appy with clerk.

Enter **Tot**.

Bolitho Ah. Tot. Can you write, Tot?

Tot I can write Tot.

Bolitho Right Tot, write Tot.

Tot Whass this?

Bolitho   Deeds of assent for Carne's bank. E signed em but there was no witness. Need a witness. There Tot. Write Tot.

Tot (*writing*)   Tot.

Billy   'arriet. I know you'll turn me down cus every other woman 'ave.

Harriet   This is a proposal?

Billy   I dun't earn much more'n what a packer get.

Harriet   A packer?

Billy   Yes.

Harriet   Thass no good to me.

Bolitho   'arriet. Sign this.

Harriet (*going*)   arn't signin nothin Mister.

Bolitho   Don't you want to own this bank?

Harriet   I can't write off the debt remember?

Bolitho   Maude, get me cheque book.

Maude   I arn't budgin Mister.

Bolitho   Dammit you're reinstated now get me cheque book. (*To* **Harriet**.) Six undred pound that do ya?

Harriet (*signing*)   Tis a start.

Bolitho   Billy. You mighta heard I took a share in a seine net over Porthleven. Rodney Rowe went to France and left a gap for Captain.

Harriet   E's givin up fishin.

Bolitho   Are ya?

Billy   Er . . .

Harriet (*signing assent forms*)   Gonna try 'is 'and at bankin.

Bolitho   See Bill? Banker. Not so bad am I.

Billy It's got bugger all to do wi'you Mister.

Bolitho I'll have to find another Captain.

Maude No ya won't.

Bolitho Got one lined up Maude?

Maude Jumbo.

Bolitho It should go to a local man. I can't be seen to favour Yorkies

Harriet She and im're gettin wed.

Bolitho Are ya Maude?

Maude Thass the way it's lookin.

Bolitho Put a different complexion on it. Let me ponder that one willya?

A huge extrusion of steam from a train as it pulls into the:

Station.
Bolitho, **Borlase**, **Tot**, **Maude**, **Billy**, **Harriet** *and*
Jumbo *meet the Army.*
Fanfare.
The transporter doors slide open and a **Company Sergeant Major** *hops out.*

CSM Companeee! Disembark!

Six hundred troops of the Royal Berkshire Regiment disembark.

Kitchen.
Mother *asleep.*
Enter **Mrs Triggs**.
She is accompanied by two undertakers with an empty coffin.

Mrs Triggs There she is. Passed away in the heat. What a day it's bin.

The undertakers prepare **Mother** *for the coffin.*

Mrs Triggs Where's Bolitha? Typical that is. Off somewhere presiding over this, openin that, toppin off. Left 'is mother dead upon the kitchen table. What about the rats?

Station.
Bolitho *inspects the troops.*

CSM   Prese-e-ent . . . arms!

Bolitho *is photographed with the top brass.*

Mother *is now laid out in the coffin.*

Mrs Triggs   Keep the lid off. She'll rot away else, like fire in this heat.

Exit undertakers, with **Mother**.

Station.

CSM   By the le-e-e-ft, qui-i-ick march!

Kitchen.
Enter **Bolitho, Maude, Jumbo, Harriet** *and* **Billy**.

Bolitho *(removing his regalia)*   Undertaker bin?

Mrs Triggs   Yes.

Bolitho *(handing regalia to* **Mrs Triggs***)*   Put this back in me study.

Exit **Mrs Triggs**.
Enter **Tot**.

Tot   Order's bin restored.

Bolitho   Thanks Tot.

Tot   I didn't approve of this action. But I'm glad they done it. These Yorkies dictate to us when to go. When I go is a matter for me, the weather, God and no bugger else. I worship in Ebeneezer. Right there by the quay. I d'walk down Jack Lane on a Sunday mornin look out across the bay and say to meself sea's like a pea on a plate, there's fish out there and a gale freshenin for tomorrer. And me right 'and d'creep up round me neck for to rip me collar off and run down on to the boat and out while I can but I dun't. And I never ave. And I d'get in chapel and I d'sit on the bench and tis like I've walked into God's open 'ands, tis safe. I'm safe. You got 'ave one day in the week when you're safe.

Enter **Mrs Triggs**.
Her face is white as snow.

Mrs Triggs There's . . .

Bolitho Now what?

Mrs Triggs – body!

Bolitho Carne?

Mrs Triggs Sitting at the rolltop!

Bolitho I thought you said Budd the undertaker came.

Mrs Triggs E did.

Bolitho Did e go again?

Mrs Triggs Yes.

Bolitho Empty-handed?

Mrs Triggs No.

Bolitho Then who did e take?

Mrs Triggs Your mother.

Bolitho Me mother?

Mrs Triggs She was laid out.

Bolitho She was fast asleep.

Mrs Triggs Not dead?

Bolitho No!

Street.
The undertakers haul the coffin on a cart down the hill.
Mother *sits up in the coffin and looks around.*

Mother Aw. This is nice. Where we goin?

The undertakers drop the coffin and run.

Kitchen
Mrs Triggs *bawls.*

Bolitho   Maude! Tot fetch me mother willya?

Exit **Tot**.
Enter **Maude**.

Bolitho   What am I gonna do with er Maude?

Maude   I know what I'd like to do with er.

Bolitho   That's not what I'm askin.

Mrs Triggs *(bawling)*   Poor ole woman! I sent er off to
Jesus!

Bolitho   She's survived worse'n that.

Mrs Triggs   Why did I do it? I shoulda gived er a prod!

Bolitho   I think it's time for you to retire. Don't argue.
I've decided. Tis final. I shall pay you a pension and
appoint Maude to take your place. All right wi'you Maude?

Maude   Yep.

Bolitho *(to* **Mrs Triggs***)*   You're forthwith discharged.

Mrs Triggs *(gathering her wits)*   Half a lifetime's devoted
service come to this. I held me own against nobility in this
kitchen. But with a fresh century comin on there's no better
time to flee the nest. I spent hour with Porky on the *Reaper*.
I never thought I'd say it 'bout a Yorkie but I liked the
man. And spindle, and Tintack. Said I could go out with
em any time on a trip.

A sharp extrusion of steam.

Cronjie *(at the wheel of the* Reaper*)*   Stir it up!

Spindle *stokes the furnace.*

Tintack   Whiffler's on!

Cronjie   What's your pressure?!

Spindle   One sixty!

Cronjie   Cast off!

Porky *unties the bow rope.*
Mrs Triggs *approaches.*

Mrs Triggs   Porky!

Porky   Mrs Triggs?

Mrs Triggs *(leaping on to the deck)*   I'm comin aboard!

Hymn   At his word the ocean yieldeth
Bounteous harvest without fail.
His hand our life that shieldeth
Through the fury of the gale.
Let us thank him
Let us thank him
For his mercies never fail . . .

Maude *resumes polishing the cutlery.*

Bolitho   I dunno Maude, I can't help feeling that nothin
but good mighta come outa this riot. What they did today
was the final desperate act of a dying age. Twas an empty
gesture. Some will ride it out and prosper from the new
era. Some will fall by the wayside. Tis a secret of success in
business to turn disaster into triumph if and when you can.
Capps will go to Plymouth. We won't see im again next
year. E'll take Uttings and Thirkles with im but will e?
They've ad their eyes opened. They are fair and decent
men and e's deeply unpopular, Capps. Could be they
isolate im and force im out. Anything is possible Maude,
don't you think?

Enter **Mother**.

Mother *(a smile on her face)*   Army's ere.

Bolitho   Dammit Mother! Good to see ya back.

Mother   I'll skip me breakfast and move on to dinner.

Bolitho   Fix er some tongue Maude, and chutney.

Maude *prepares dinner for* **Mother**.

Mother *picks at her food.*

A loud banging on the door.

Bolitho (*locking the doors*) What I do know is we got the nineteen undreds comin up and there's countless opportunities for businessmen like me. Where one door shuts another two open up ... broccoli's took a dive in this heat, plant mangles! Tin drops, invest in pilchards.

He sits at the table and resumes his dinner.

Tomorra's another day Mother Eat your chutney.

Mother *picks at her food. A loud banging on the door.*

Bolitho Now what? Oo's there!?

Capps (*off*) Capps! Open up!

Bolitho Goddammit!

Mother Oo is it?

Bolitho Capps Mother.

Mother Capps?

Bolitho Yorky merchant.

Mother Is e frisky?

Bolitho Capps? Frisky? Yes Mother.

He opens the door.

Mr Capps ... meet me mother ...

The lights fade.

End.

A SELECTED LIST OF
METHUEN MODERN PLAYS

☐ CLOSER	Patrick Marber	£6.99
☐ THE BEAUTY QUEEN OF LEENANE	Martin McDonagh	£6.99
☐ A SKULL IN CONNEMARA	Martin McDonagh	£6.99
☐ THE LONESOME WEST	Martin McDonagh	£6.99
☐ THE CRIPPLE OF INISHMAAN	Martin McDonagh	£6.99
☐ THE STEWARD OF CHRISTENDOM	Sebastian Barry	£6.99
☐ SHOPPING AND F***ING	Mark Ravenhill	£6.99
☐ FAUST (FAUST IS DEAD)	Mark Ravenhill	£5.99
☐ POLYGRAPH	Robert Lepage and Marie Brassard	£6.99
☐ BEAUTIFUL THING	Jonathan Harvey	£6.99
☐ MEMORY OF WATER & FIVE KINDS OF SILENCE	Shelagh Stephenson	£7.99
☐ WISHBONES	Lucinda Coxon	£6.99
☐ BONDAGERS & THE STRAW CHAIR	Sue Glover	£9.99
☐ SOME VOICES & PALE HORSE	Joe Penhall	£7.99
☐ KNIVES IN HENS	David Harrower	£6.99
☐ BOYS' LIFE & SEARCH AND DESTROY	Howard Korder	£8.99
☐ THE LIGHTS	Howard Korder	£6.99
☐ SERVING IT UP & A WEEK WITH TONY	David Eldridge	£8.99
☐ INSIDE TRADING	Malcolm Bradbury	£6.99
☐ MASTERCLASS	Terrence McNally	£5.99
☐ EUROPE & THE ARCHITECT	David Greig	£7.99
☐ BLUE MURDER	Peter Nichols	£6.99
☐ BLASTED & PHAEDRA'S LOVE	Sarah Kane	£7.99

• All Methuen Drama books are available through mail order or from your local bookshop.

Please send cheque/eurocheque/postal order (sterling only) Access, Visa, Mastercard, Diners Card, Switch or Amex.

☐ ☐ ☐ ☐ ☐ ☐ ☐ ☐ ☐ ☐ ☐ ☐ ☐ ☐ ☐ ☐

Expiry Date:_____ Signature: _____

Please allow 75 pence per book for post and packing U.K.
Overseas customers please allow £1.00 per copy for post and packing.

ALL ORDERS TO:

Methuen Books, Books by Post, TBS Limited, The Book Service, Colchester Road, Frating Green, Colchester, Essex CO7 7DW.

NAME: _____

ADDRESS: _____

_____

_____

Please allow 28 days for delivery. Please tick box if you do not wish to receive any additional information   ☐

Prices and availability subject to change without notice.

For a Complete Catalogue of Methuen Drama titles
write to:

Methuen Publishing Limited
215 Vauxhall Bridge Road
London SW1V 1EJ